The History of the Democratic Party: A Political Primer

By Charles River Editors

About Charles River Editors

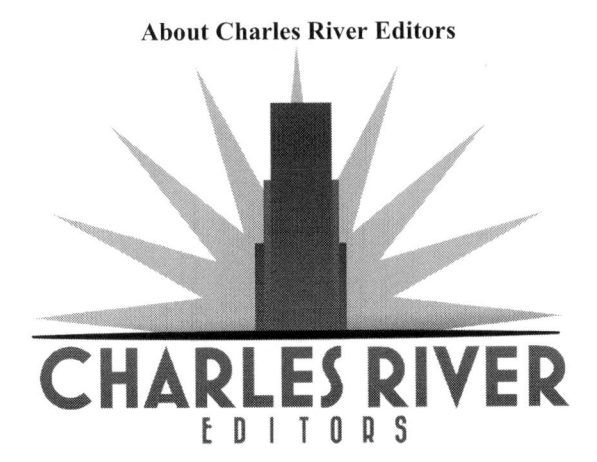

Charles River Editors was founded by Harvard and MIT alumni to provide superior editing and original writing services, with the expertise to create digital content for publishers across a vast range of subject matter. In addition to providing original digital content for third party publishers, Charles River Editors republishes civilization's greatest literary works, bringing them to a new generation via ebooks.

Visit charlesrivereditors.com for more information.

Introduction

The Democratic Party

"I hope the two wings of the Democratic Party may flap together." – William Jennings Bryan

As the oldest political party in the United States, the Democratic Party has been one of the nation's major political parties for over 150 years, and diverse men and ideas have fallen under its tent since the 19th century. Today the Democrats are generally viewed as proponents of a strong, centralized federal government, and yet the forerunner of the modern party was none other than Thomas Jefferson, the man most associated with states' rights and limited government.

With its Jeffersonian background, the party championed farmers, and Andrew Jackson's populist era made the Party home to urban workers and new immigrants. Eventually sectional splits weakened the Democrats, and when the fledgling Republican Party took power under Abraham Lincoln in 1861, it ushered in an era in which the Democrats only elected 2 presidents over a 70 year span. However, Reconstruction ensured that the Democrats maintained an almost unbreakable level of support in the old Confederate states, and they used the Solid South to wield power in Congress for decades.

150 years after the Civil War, the Democratic Party's current voting bloc (strongly reliant on minorities) and their base of power (the Northeast and Midwest) are completely different than the 19th century's incarnation. Its platform has also been completely revamped. Both of those reversals are byproducts of Franklin Roosevelt's New Deal and Lyndon B. Johnson's Great Society, which continue to be the pillars on which the Democrats' current platform rests.

The History of the Democratic Party looks back at the historical narrative of the Democrats, including their key leaders, important changes and events, and the Party's current political platform. Along with pictures, you will learn about the Democratic Party like you never have before, in no time at all.

Chapter 1: Before the Democratic Party

When he emerged from the Constitutional Convention in 1787, Benjamin Franklin was stopped and asked what the men writing the new government had decided upon.

"A republic," he answered, "if you can keep it."

More than 200 years later, the Republic has indeed endured. Yet one of the most common complaints here today is that the Founders would be shocked at the partisan and gridlock that consume so much of American politics today. In fact, the founders might not be surprised at all. The system of government created in Philadelphia was in many ways designed to create such gridlock.

In the Federalist Papers that were written to encourage support for the new Constitution, James Madison wrote that the system of checks and balances created by the founders would pit "faction against faction." Perhaps another word for this phenomenon is "gridlock."

The Founding Fathers saw this as healthy and good for the young Republic. They feared mob rule and wanted to make government a thoughtful and slow process. Hence, the design of the government separated powers; and the legislative branch was divided into two parts so that legislation could not move easily.

As Hamilton wrote in Federalist #31, "A government ought to contain in itself every power requisite to the full accomplishment of the objects committed to its care, and to the complete execution of the trusts for which it is responsible, free from every other control but a regard to the public good and to the sense of the people." In essence, the founders wanted a government big enough to get things done, but not too big that it forgot it worked for the people.

As a result of this design, the creation of political parties was inevitable. Any time an issue is debated there are typically two opposing sides, and the "factions" that Madison wrote about would eventually organize formally and name themselves. For the people who today gather under the Democratic Party banner, the man to whom they trace their lineage is Thomas Jefferson.

Jefferson

In the late 19th century, a debate raged in Europe and America about the goal of government. In the American Revolution, the colonists waged war for a specific reason: they were being taxed and yet had no say in Parliament. Despite what Thomas Paine wrote at the time, many of the American revolutionaries weren't trying to make the world anew: they just wanted lower taxes and a vote in government. This has led some historians to label the American Revolution a "conservative" revolution.

A few years later in France, a very different kind of battle broke out. In the French Revolution, seemingly no limits existed to the goals of the revolutionaries. Instead, a war ensued that was designed to achieve "liberty, equality and fraternity," a far cry from "taxation without representation."

Ironically, Jefferson found himself in Paris as the Revolution began, and from the start, he found himself in complete sympathy with the French Revolution. When he returned to the United States to serve as President Washington's Secretary of State, he brought with him a renewed disdain for monarchy and a rekindled fire for democracy. Meanwhile, he found himself serving in Washington's cabinet alongside Alexander Hamilton, the Secretary of Treasury. Hamilton was appalled by the excesses of the French Revolution and thought America could do worse than to copy the British policy of establishing a national debt and creating a national bank.

Since Washington frequently sided with Hamilton, Jefferson was concerned about Hamilton's influence on the President, but he was not the only one. As early as 1791, Jefferson began consorting with James Madison of Virginia and Aaron Burr and DeWitt Clinton of New York to form an allied opposition to Hamilton's policies. Under Jefferson's leadership, they organized a party that came to be called the Democratic-Republicans, which opposed Hamilton's understanding of a flexible constitution and his advocacy for a strong federal government. They were often simply referred to as Jeffersonians.

On almost every major issue of the Washington Presidency, the Secretary of State and the Secretary of the Treasury had clashed. Jefferson often felt slighted by both the President and Hamilton, who tended to side with one another. This came up in both domestic and foreign policy. Hamilton's area of expertise was economics, so Jefferson could justify Washington's siding with Hamilton on taxes and banking. But on foreign policy – particularly on war between France and Great Britain in 1793 – Washington again sided with Hamilton, despite Jefferson being the Secretary of State. Jefferson and his allies supported France in the conflict while Hamilton supported Great Britain; Washington decided on neutrality.

In response to the mobilization of the Democratic-Republicans, Hamilton didn't sit idly by. He became the intellectual driving force of another party, the Federalists, and gained crucial allies like John Adams to join his cause in support of a strong central government. The two parties mobilized in often-vitriolic ways, lambasting their opponents in newspapers throughout the country.

Hamilton

Thus was formed the nation's first Party System. One party, the Federalists, was led by Alexander Hamilton and supported a strong federal government. Its supporters were primarily Northern and were frequently attached to business or capitalist interests. The other party was the Democratic-Republicans, led by Thomas Jefferson, who supported more agrarian interests and preferred to reserve more power for the states. The Democratic-Republicans garnered most of their support from Southern farmers.

Hamilton and Jefferson would clash and compete for Washington's influence so frequently that Jefferson felt himself forced out of the cabinet and resigned in 1793, at the beginning of Washington's second term as President

Madison's predication of "faction against faction" had first played out as Jefferson against Hamilton, and in this initial bit of gridlock, the outlines of the Democratic Party began to emerge.

Chapter 2: The Democratic-Republicans

In many ways, Jefferson seems a strange founder of a party that has long claimed to be devoted to the interests of the working class. The Sage of Monticello was anything but working class. Sophisticated and urbane, Jefferson spoke several languages, enjoyed wine from overseas and was not shy about using slave labor to build and rebuild his estate.

One of the benefits of a life of luxury was Jefferson had time to read, think and write, and with that his mind was an ocean that roared with waves of ideas and vision. To Jefferson, America had little in common with aristocratic England. Instead, he viewed America as a "natural aristocracy" where ordinary people could do extraordinary things; he wanted to create a nation of "yeoman farmers" where people ran their own farms and their own affairs.

Jefferson feared that this might not be possible if Hamilton's economic program were adopted, especially with the formation of a national bank. Southerners thought it gave excessive powers to the federal government at the expense of the states. Jefferson had other reasons to oppose the bill; always a fan of agriculture, Jefferson saw the bank as no friend of farmers. He thought it was geared exclusively towards helping urban businessmen improve their fortunes. To some extent, Hamilton wouldn't disagree with this assessment; he thought the United States was destined not to be a Jeffersonian agrarian nation, but a large industrial one.

And so the Democratic-Republican Party, as it was then called, began as a limited government party. It traced its roots to classical liberalism and it acknowledged that every man is endowed with natural rights. Above all, Jefferson's party would fight hard against big government and big money and stand firm for states' rights. Meanwhile, Hamilton and John Adams belonged to the Federalist Party, which favored a strong national government, trade ties to England, and a centralized bank. America now had its first two organized political parties.

Jefferson soon got to try out his brand of politics as the third president of the United States, only to learn what all presidents eventually do. Sometimes a philosophy works much better in theory than in practice. When presented with the chance to execute the Louisiana Purchase, Jefferson briefly overlooked his limited government principles and doubled the size of the young country.

Still, even today's American dialogue focuses heavily on the balance of power between state and federal government. In fact, the current size of the federal government has been the foremost political issue in the country's most recent elections. Jefferson ensured that the strain that supported stronger states would live on strongly in rural America, because he intertwined the virtues of small, local governments and an agrarian life style, and the appeal of states rights still lives on in rural America today. At its base, Jefferson's political philosophy trusted the broad masses to govern themselves. Such trust is now a defining cornerstone of American democracy.

When Jefferson assumed the Presidency in 1800, he did so after 12 years of Federalist government, and it was not clear that the United States would prefer a course of government that trusted a broad democracy. Moments like the passage of the Alien and Sedition Acts suggest that the United States might have limited the rights guaranteed in the Bill of Rights. Jefferson changed that, and in doing so undid the first 12 years of American political history, and ensured that a more limited, trusting and democratic view of government prevailed in the United States until the Civil War. After Jefferson left the office of President, both of his successors – who both served two terms – were devout Democratic-Republicans. Presidents Madison and Monroe further ensured that Jeffersonianism would dominate American political discourse.

Chapter 3: Jacksonian Democrats

Andrew Jackson

In the search for a successor to President James Monroe, the Democratic-Republican Party split. The group that was still devoted to Jeffersonian principles became known simply as "Democrats" and was led in the 1824 presidential election by Andrew Jackson.

The Election of 1824, however, proved to be a watershed in American political history, opening the doors to the present-day two party system. Jackson initially had trouble securing the nomination of the Democratic-Republicans, because the Congressional Caucus nominated

William Crawford, the sitting Secretary of the Treasury. Jackson may have been a military hero who was popular with the country, but the nomination process did not involve citizens voting yet, and Jackson now faced an entrenched politician.

Luckily for Jackson, many within the party thought that that method of selection was undemocratic, and that Crawford's nomination was illegitimate. Other candidates thus jumped in the race, believing Crawford stood no chance of winning. Secretary of State John Quincy Adams threw his hat into the race, as did the "Great Compromiser", Henry Clay of Kentucky, and, briefly, Secretary of War John C. Calhoun, who dropped out after deciding he wanted to be Vice President instead. And finally, Andrew Jackson also decided to run for the White House. Jackson was now running against several Cabinet members and one of the Lions of the Senate.

All of the candidates were members of the Democratic-Republican Party, though John Quincy Adams appealed to the former Federalists in New England thanks to his famous father. On Election Day, Andrew Jackson won a plurality of the electoral votes, but not the needed majority. Quincy Adams solidly won the Northeast, Clay won some of the modern-day Midwest, Crawford won a few Southern States, and Jackson won all of the remaining states. He had earned 99 electoral votes to Quincy Adams' 84, but 131 were needed to win the election.

For the first time since 1800, the election of the President was sent to the House of Representatives. There, Clay endorsed Quincy Adams, giving his electors to him. Quincy Adams thus won the Presidency and immediately appointed Clay Secretary of State, which appeared to be the most basic quid-pro-quo. Andrew Jackson was dismayed, and he and his supporters labeled the deal a "corrupt bargain" indicative of insider politics and not populism. Jackson and his supporters vowed there would be a rematch in 1828.

John Quincy Adams

In some sense, Jackson's defeat in 1824 only emboldened his case for the Presidency. As Quincy Adams went on to increase the role of the federal government in the economy, Jackson contended that he governed like a Federalist. To Jackson, Quincy Adams's presidency symbolized the transfer of tax wealth from the common people to the elites. Besides, Jackson could also make the argument that Quincy Adams's presidency was the result of an unjust bargain of power among D.C. elites anyway. Jackson hoped to represent the common people in the White House, and with that he ran for the Presidency again in 1828.

In 1825, the Tennessee Legislature quickly re-nominated Jackson for President just months after his defeat, setting the stage for a rematch in three years. But in order to smooth the process for Jackson's candidacy, Jackson and his supporters side-stepped the national Democratic-Republican Party and created their own political organization: the Democrats. The Tennessee Senator and national military hero made an odd choice for his running mate, selecting sitting Vice President John C. Calhoun. No nominating caucus was held for John Quincy Adams, though he did run for reelection as a "National Republican." In essence, the one party that had ruled the country for nearly 30 years destroyed itself picking a president in 1824, bringing back a national two-party system.

Having resigned from the Senate after the Election of 1824, Jackson spent most of Quincy Adams's presidency on the campaign trail. With the help of powerful American politicians, including Martin Van Buren, Andrew Jackson essentially remodeled the old Democratic-Republican Party and reassembled much of its coalition under the Democratic Party. Meanwhile, Quincy Adams found himself limited to the constituency that his father attracted, the old Federalists of New England. To fight back, Quincy Adams supporters labeled Jackson a "jackass," but Jackson liked the term, accepted it, and gave his new political party a mascot that lasts to this day.

On Election Day, the results mirrored those of the days when the Federalist Party was in its last throes. Jackson won handily, carrying all states except those in New England and some in the mid-Atlantic. He won 178 electoral votes to Quincy Adams's 83, ensuring there would be no need for backroom deals to pick a president.

Jackson had just reached the pinnacle of power, but his election was not all fun and excitement. As the "jackass" label suggested, the Election of 1828 included some bitter politicking, and the two sides attacked from every possible angle. During the race, supporters of Quincy Adams seized on the fact Jackson and his wife had gotten married before her divorce from her previous marriage was finalized. Rachel was attacked as a promiscuous woman who believed in bigamy by newspapers supportive of Quincy Adams during the race. When Rachel died of bronchial problems and heart trouble just five days after he was elected, Jackson accused his opponents of causing her undue stress and a premature death.

Regardless, Jackson was inaugurated as the seventh President of the United States on March 4th, 1829. On his very first day in office, Jackson's uniqueness as a President was apparent. All prior Presidents had come from aristocratic backgrounds and were afforded quality educations. This was not the case with Jackson; unlike his predecessors, Jackson was a common man from the backcountry of the old Southwest.

Jackson's support for the common man was symbolic and substantive. Previous inaugurations resembled the black tie affairs that accompany inaugurations today, but Jackson's inauguration ceremony demonstrated his background. On his first day in office, he opened the executive mansion to the public so that anyone could enter and celebrate the inauguration. When common citizens were invited to the party, an uncontrollable mob broke into the White House and destroyed expensive china while celebrating. Fist fights also broke out in the upheaval. It was a very different type of celebration than any the White House had hosted.

Perhaps the greatest policy challenge Jackson faced came from the Second Bank of the United States. The bank, a part of Hamilton's vision of a strong centralized government, had been authorized during the Madison administration, but there was a hitch: the bank had only been authorized for 20 years. Jackson worked successfully to have the bank's charter rescinded. "The bank is trying to kill me," he once said to his vice president, "but I will kill it." He did, and the Jeffersonian dream of an agricultural republic had returned. "Fear not," he once said in a neat summation of his populist views, "the people may be deluded for a moment, but cannot be corrupted."

Yet one of the unintended consequences of the Jeffersonian vision that the Democrats still adhered to was the fervor that was attached to states' rights. At that time in American history, many if not most people thought of themselves as citizens of their state first. A person in Virginia, for example, would likely call himself a Virginian before he would call himself an America. This may have seemed harmless at the time, but Jackson, to his eternal credit, recognized the danger.

In 1832, the issue of tariffs on the importation of foreign goods nearly ripped the nation apart and ignited a civil war three decades before one actually occurred. Four years earlier, a tariff had been passed that taxed the importation of manufactured goods, many of which came from the industries of Great Britain. This tax was passed with the intention of protecting industry in the Northern states from competition from foreign industrial countries. The South, however, was less industrial and relied on the export of cotton; by reducing the competitiveness of British industry, the economy there was less able to afford to import cotton from the United States. To the South, the protective tariffs were one-sided and supported the North at the expense of the

South, and the region loudly opposed them.

In 1832, a new tariff was passed that was less harsh than the one from 1828, but the South still opposed the bill. In response, South Carolina began to consider passing an ordinance of nullification, prohibiting the tariff within its borders. Vice President Calhoun encouraged the act, and supported its Constitutionality. On November 19th, South Carolina adopted the Ordinance of Nullification, overturning the tariffs of 1828 and 1832 within its borders. It also vowed that any attempts to enforce the law within its borders would lead to the state's secession from the Union.

Modern American jurisprudence has ensured that federal laws are supreme to state laws when they are in conflict, but South Carolina's assertion that it had the ability to nullify a federal law dated all the way back to the "Kentucky and Virginia Resolutions", which were drafted by Jefferson and Madison. Together, the two drafted the first major political documents advocating the rights of the states to nullify federal law that the states believed was unconstitutional. Citing this doctrine of "nullification," various states in both the North and South asserted the states' rights to consider federal laws invalid. The Resolutions sought to nullify the Alien and Sedition Acts within those states back in the late 18th century, Northern states debated nullification during the War of 1812, and in 1860, Southern states would take nullification one step further to outright secession, leading to the Civil War.

Amid the crisis, Jackson was reelected by a wide margin. He did not, however, win the state of South Carolina, which nominated its own candidate, John Floyd of the Nullifier Party. Within less than a week of his reelection, Jackson stated his position on the Nullification Crisis. He said that John Calhoun's doctrine of Nullification was an "impractical absurdity," defied Constitutional law, and was tantamount to treason. Jackson, himself a Southerner, spoke a prophetic warning: "The Constitution... forms a *government* not a league... To say that any State may at pleasure secede from the Union is to say that the United States is not a nation."

Thus, President Jackson absolutely denied that a state had the right to overturn federal law, and he committed the U.S. military to quelling any attempts to do that in South Carolina. Ten days later, Vice President Calhoun resigned, having won a seat in the U.S. Senate, and he continued to support Nullification throughout the crisis.

Calhoun

To give added support to his demands, the President asked Congress for an authorization to use force in January of 1833. On February 20th, Congress passed the Force Bill, known as the "Bloody Bill," which authorized Jackson to use military force in South Carolina. Jackson went beyond this, vowing to personally murder John C. Calhoun and "hang him high as Hamen." Such belligerent militance was typical of President Jackson.

Eventually Congress managed a compromise in March, authored by the "Great Compromiser" Henry Clay himself. The new bill reduced all tariffs for a ten year period and was signed into law on March 15th. South Carolina revoked its Ordinance of Nullification, though it nullified the Force Bill in the same act. Regardless, the Nullification Crisis was over.

Jackson believed in the "natural aristocracy" of Jefferson and shared his faith in states' rights; but he foresaw that the latter could lead to conflict and even disunion.

Chapter 4: 1850s Politics and the Election of 1860

Throughout the 1850s, American politicians tried to sort out the nation's intractable issues. In an attempt to organize the center of North America – Kansas and Nebraska – without offsetting the slave-free balance, Senator Stephen Douglas of Illinois proposed the Kansas-Nebraska Act. The Kansas-Nebraska Act eliminated the Missouri Compromise line of 1820, which the Compromise of 1850 had maintained. The Missouri Compromise had stipulated that states north of the boundary line determined in that bill would be free, and that states south of it *could* have slavery. This was essential to maintaining the balance of slave and free states in the Union. The Kansas-Nebraska Act, however, ignored the line completely and proposed that all new territories be organized by popular sovereignty. Settlers could vote whether they wanted their state to be slave or free.

Stephen Douglas, "The Little Giant"

Whigs and Free Soilers were aghast over the Kansas-Nebraska Act. How could Congress now – theoretically – allow slavery to extend into *any* unsettle territory? This strictly violated some of the Whigs' dearest held principle that the further extension of slavery should not extend further. Whigs and Free Soilers in the North quickly coalesced against the "Slave Power." They felt Southern influence in Washington had gone too far and held the government in a stranglehold. This coalescence first became known as the "anti-Nebraska" group, but quickly vowed to form a new political party dedicated to keeping the Western territories free from slavery. They called themselves the Republicans.

Although destined to be forever associated with the Republican Party, Abraham Lincoln remained a Whig for some time. He agreed with the Republicans on the issue of Kansas-Nebraska, but wasn't yet convinced that the Party of Henry Clay was on its last legs. Instead, Lincoln focused his efforts on Democrat Stephen Douglas, the "Little Giant." The day after a major speech given by Douglas in which he defended his Kansas-Nebraska Act, Lincoln gave a speech known as the "Peoria Speech." In his speech, Lincoln laid out his opinion on slavery, a position he would keep only until the very last months of his Presidency. It can be summed up best by Lincoln himself: "I wish to make and to keep the distinction between the existing institution, and the extension of it, so broad, and so clear, that no honest man can misunderstand me." Lincoln conceded the South's constitutional right to the maintenance of slavery in their states, but he firmly pushed back on the idea that it needed to be extended beyond where it already existed. Lincoln said he thought slavery would die out on its own with time, and that this was the position of the Founders. Federal intervention was not needed to abolish slavery.

Popular sovereignty was wrong because it allowed anyone to bring slaves into new territory, and thereby extend the institution into new states. Its extension - *anywhere* – was what Lincoln wanted to disallow.

Republicans throughout the North had gone through great pains to patch together a coalition of Whigs, "Know-Nothings" and Free Soilers. Having achieved success, the Republicans were on the verge of becoming the new majority party in the North. With his speech, Lincoln was now considered a leader of the anti-Nebraska men in Illinois.

When popular sovereignty became the standard in Kansas and Nebraska, the primary result was that thousands of zealous pro-slavery and anti-slavery advocates both moved to Kansas to influence the vote, creating a dangerous (and ultimately deadly) mix. Numerous attacks took place between the two sides, and many pro-slavery Missourians organized attacks on Kansas towns just across the border.

The best known abolitionist in Bleeding Kansas was a middle aged man named John Brown. A radical abolitionist, Brown organized a small band of like-minded followers and fought with the armed groups of pro-slavery men in Kansas for several months, including a notorious incident known as the Pottawatomie Massacre, in which Brown's supporters murdered five men. Over 50 people died before John Brown left the territory, which ultimately entered the Union as a free state in 1859.

John Brown

Now a veteran of the Native American frontier conflicts, from 1855 to 1861 First Lieutenant Stuart was given a leadership position in defusing "Bleeding Kansas" (or the "Border War"), the violent political confrontations between anti-slavery "Free-Staters" (like John Brown) and pro-slavery "Border Ruffians" that took place in the Kansas Territory and neighboring towns of

Missouri, and ended with the "Pottawatomie Massacre."

On July 29, 1857, Stuart demonstrated his knack for initiative and bravery during the Cheyenne uprising known as the Battle of Solomon's River in present day Kansas. According to reports, after his commander, Colonel Sumner, ordered a "drawn sabers" charge against a band of Cheyenne who were firing a barrage of arrows, Stuart and three other lieutenants chased one Cheyenne down, who Stuart then shot in the thigh. The Native American, however, turned and fired at Stuart with a flintlock, striking him directly in the chest, but doing little actual damage. By the time Stuart returned to Fort Leavenworth that September to reunite with his family, word of his courage and exceptional leadership abilities preceded him.

After his activities in Kansas, John Brown spent the next few years raising money in New England, which would bring him into direct contact with important abolitionist leaders, including Frederick Douglass. Brown had previously organized a small raiding party that succeeded in raiding a Missouri farm and freeing 11 slaves, but he set his sights on far larger objectives. In 1859, Brown began to set a new plan in motion that he hoped would create a full scale slave uprising in the South. Brown's plan relied on raiding Harpers Ferry, a strategically located armory in western Virginia that had been the main federal arms depot after the Revolution. Given its proximity to the South, Brown hoped to seize thousands of rifles and move them south, gathering slaves and swelling his numbers as he went. The slaves would then be armed and ready to help free more slaves, inevitably fighting Southern militias along the way.

In recognition of how important escaped slave Frederick Douglass had become among abolitionists, Brown attempted to enlist the support of Douglass by informing him of the plans. While Douglass didn't blow the whistle on Brown, he told Brown that violence would only further enrage the South, and slaveholders might only retaliate further against slaves with devastating consequences. Instead of helping Brown, Douglass dissuaded freed blacks from joining Brown's group because he believed it was doomed to fail.

Despite that, in July 1859, Brown traveled to Harper's Ferry under an assumed name and waited for his recruits, but he struggled to get even 20 people to join him. Rather than call off the plan, however, Brown went ahead with it. That fall, Brown and his men used hundreds of rifles to seize the armory at Harper's Ferry, but the plan went haywire from the start, and word of his attack quickly spread. Local pro-slavery men formed a militia and pinned Brown and his men down while they were still at the armory.

After being called to Harpers Ferry, Robert E. Lee took decisive command of a troop of marines stationed there, surrounded the arsenal, and gave Brown the opportunity to surrender peaceably. When Brown refused, Lee ordered the doors be broken down and Brown taken captive, an affair that reportedly lasted just three minutes. A few of Brown's men were killed, but Brown was taken alive. Lee earned acclaim for accomplishing this task so quickly and efficiently.

The fallout from John Brown's raid on Harpers Ferry was intense. Southerners had long suspected that abolitionists hoped to arm the slaves and use violence to abolish slavery, and Brown's raid seemed to confirm that. Meanwhile, much of the northern press praised Brown for his actions. In the South, conspiracy theories ran wild about who had supported the raid, and many believed prominent abolitionist Republicans had been behind the raid as well. On the day of his execution, Brown wrote, "I, John Brown, am now quite *certain* that the crimes of this *guilty land* will never be purged away but with *blood.* I had, as I now think vainly, flattered myself that without very much bloodshed it might be done."

The man in command of the troops present at Brown's hanging was none other than Thomas Jonathan Jackson, who was ordered to Charlestown in November 1859. After Brown's hanging, the future Stonewall Jackson began to believe war was inevitable, but he wrote his aunt, "I think we have great reason for alarm, but my trust is in God; and I cannot think that He will permit the madness of men to interfere so materially with the Christian labors of this country at home and abroad."

In the 1856 election, the Republican nominee, John Fremont, ultimately lost to the Democrat James Buchanan, but the Party came in second, a remarkable showing for a brand new political party.

Going into the Republican Convention in May of 1860, the Republicans were hopeful. The Democratic Party, partly because of Stephen Douglas, was deeply divided over slavery, and it had broken into a Northern and Southern faction. By dividing their votes, they were likely handing over the presidency to a Republican Party that would barely win a plurality across the nation. Sensing opportunity, the Republicans were careful in selecting their candidate. Many delegates considered the frontrunner, William H. Seward, to be too radical. With a divided electorate, there were fears that Seward's radicalism might lose the Midwest for the Republicans.

At the Convention, Seward's support maintained steady throughout the rounds of voting. Lincoln polled a surprising second place on the first ballot. He gradually picked up votes from other Midwestern candidates until he was selected as the Republican Party's Presidential nominee on the third ballot. Hanibal Hamlin of Maine was nominated as the Vice Presidential nominee.

Lincoln had essentially been chosen for his moderate stance on slavery. Unlike many other viable Republican contenders, Lincoln was less likely to alienate valuable "battleground" states like Illinois, Indiana and Ohio. At the same time, the more staunchly abolitionist Northeast would have no better alternative.

Throughout the fall, the campaign broiled on. As was customary, Lincoln did no active campaigning. Presidential candidates in the mid-1800's did not campaign on their own behalf; surrogates did the work for them. His supporters portrayed Lincoln as a man of great integrity from humble origins. Opponents conjured up the image of a radical Black Republican. Evidently, such language sold well in the South. By mid-summer, talk of Southern secession if Lincoln were elected was commonplace. Lincoln himself took none of this chatter seriously: he thought it to be nothing more than the usual political sensationalism.

Lincoln in 1860

Nevertheless, the election of 1860 was held under extraordinary circumstances, and the results were equally unprecedented. Four candidates competed, and each of the candidates won some electoral votes. While the Republicans nominated Abraham Lincoln, the Democrats nominated Stephen Douglas, the Southern Democrats chose John C. Breckinridge and the Constitutional Union Party selected John Bell of Tennessee as its nominee. The Constitutional Union Party was compromised of former Know-Nothings and Whigs in the middle states of Kentucky, Tennessee and Virginia who advocated compromise and unity on the issue of slavery.

The race was so fractured that Lincoln only appeared on the ballot in five slave states: Virginia, Kentucky, Maryland, Delaware and Missouri. In Virginia, Lincoln only won about 1% of the vote, and in all the other slave states where Lincoln was on the ballot he finished no better than third. Lincoln won only two counties out all 996 counties in the 15 slave states.

On election night, Lincoln and the Republicans won decisively in the Electoral College, with 180 of the 303 votes cast and 152 needed for a majority. In the popular vote, however, Lincoln only garnered 39%, but came out nearly half a million votes ahead of his next nearest competitor, Stephen Douglas. In the Electoral College, Douglas only won 12 votes with a single state – Missouri. Lincoln swept the North, Breckinridge took the South, and Bell won most of the middle. The results reflected the great regional divide: the nation was set for Civil War.

By the Fall of 1860, everyone could see the "war-cloud" on the horizon. With the election of Republican candidate Abraham Lincoln as president on November 6, 1860, many Southerners considered it the final straw. Someone they knew as a "Black Republican", leader of a party whose central platform was to stop the spread of slavery to new states, was now set to be inaugurated as President in March.

Throughout the fall and winter of 1860, Southern calls for secession became increasingly serious. In a last-ditched effort to save the Union, Kentucky's Senator John Crittenden tried to assume the stateliness of his predecessor Henry Clay. Crittenden, however, proved to be no Henry Clay: his proposal that a Constitutional Amendment reinstate the Missouri Compromise line and extend it to the Pacific failed. President Buchanan supported the measure, but President-Elect Lincoln said he refused to allow the further expansion of slavery under any conditions.

The Crittenden Compromise failed on December 18. Two days later, South Carolina seceded from the Union. President Buchanan sat on his hands, believing the Southern states had no right to secede, but that the Federal government had no effective power to prevent secession. In January, Mississippi, Florida, Alabama, Georgia, Louisiana and Kansas followed South Carolina's lead. The Confederacy was formed on February 4th, in Montgomery, Alabama, with former Secretary of War Jefferson Davis as its President. On February 23rd, Texas joined the Confederacy.

Chapter 5: Out of Power

After the war and after Lincoln's assassination, the Republican Party enjoyed a long period of dominance as it perpetuated the narrative that it was the party that had saved the Union. Although Democrat Andrew Johnson inherited the presidency (and was nearly impeached by Radical Republicans), and Grover Cleveland was elected twice, it would not be until Woodrow Wilson's election in 1912, did the Democrats present the country with another iconic figure.

During Reconstruction, the Democrats continued to suffer electoral defeat because they were synonymous in the North with being against the Civil War. However, down South they were boosted by white Southerners' resentment of Reconstruction and natural hostility to the Republican Party. Before Reconstruction was over, the Democrats had control of the House of Representatives.

With the Solid South as their base of support, buoyed by the widespread disenfranchisement of blacks in the late 19th century, the Democrats could rely on the South to make them competitive in elections. The Democrats also became gradually more competitive in the mid-Atlantic and lower Midwest, allowing New York Governor Grover Cleveland to win the presidency in 1884 and 1892. Cleveland was the leader of a wing of the party known as the Bourbon Democrats, who represented the business interests instead of the agrarians in the South. Still, the Bourbon Democrats had enough in common with their Solid South compatriots, including opposition to imperialism and overseas expansion. The Bourbon Democrats also were reformists, acting out against the corruption of city bosses like Boss Tweed and Tammany Hall in New York.

It was Woodrow Wilson, however, who represented a new development in Democratic Party thought. Where Jefferson argued on behalf of the yeoman farmer and Jackson fought off big government, Wilson decided to *use* government power to help working class people. This differed in important ways from the Hamilton-Jefferson dispute. Hamilton thought of government as a tool for creating credit and laying the foundation for business. Wilson tweaked that and began using government as a tool to help workers. During his administration, laws were passed to fund farmers, protect railroad workers and outlaw child labor.

Perhaps Wilson's greatest legacy was his elevation of the presidency to a status as first among equals with the other branches of government. He made the presidency the central focus of the government for most Americans. Most tellingly, he became the first president since John Adams to deliver the State of the Union in person, which allowed him to capture the attention of the Congress and the nation and set the agenda.

Wilson

After Wilson, three consecutive Republican terms ended with the Great Depression and the election of Franklin Delano Roosevelt. The Roosevelt administration is where the modern Democratic Party really began.

Chapter 6: The FDR Years

Franklin Delano Roosevelt

When the Great Depression struck, Republican President Herbert Hoover attempted without success to fix the economy on a national level, while New York Governor Franklin D. Roosevelt used the Depression to build nationwide stature. President Hoover and the Republicans continued to rely on market economics, expecting the economy to end its bust and turn itself around, but Roosevelt began to advocate a relatively novel idea – that the economy would not fix itself but needed help from government.

Among Roosevelt's major reforms as Governor was the creation of an unemployment relief agency. He also created numerous other social programs aimed at relieving poverty and stimulating the economy, including an old-age pension bill that served as a model for Social Security. Many of these proposals served as precursors for the later New Deal. They, also, however, increased the state's budget deficit, from $15 million when Roosevelt entered office, to $90 million by the time he left.

With the economy still cratering, Democrats were especially hungry for victory in 1932. The Democrats had only won the White House four times since the Civil War, and each time only because of unusual or precarious circumstances. With the Great Depression deepening, the party saw an opening to shift the American political paradigm in its favor.

Many looked to FDR to carry the banner of change, but not all Democrats were initially convinced. Southern Democrats were especially wary of nominating Roosevelt, ironically because of his supposed pro-Catholic leanings. Roosevelt's early antagonistic relationship with Irish voters in New York belied that belief, and his support of Catholicism had been tepid and political in nature, making it a relatively easy issue for him to surmount. On the fourth ballot at the party's Chicago convention, Roosevelt was selected as the nominee, with Speaker of the House John Nance Garner as his running mate. Until 1932, tradition dictated that a candidate accept a nomination in writing only. Roosevelt broke this tradition, flew to Chicago, and told the convention "I pledge to you, I pledge to myself, to a new deal for the American people." That phrase would define the first half of his Presidency.

During the 1932 presidential election, the governor of New York promised the American people a "New Deal." But FDR provided few details on the campaign trail. Roosevelt was a master politician. Oliver Wendell Holmes joked that FDR possessed a "second-rate intellect but a first-rate temperament." This temperament allowed him to skillfully navigate the political waters of Washington.

On Election Day, Roosevelt won handily. In one of the biggest margins in electoral history, Roosevelt carried 472 electoral votes to Herbert Hoover's 59, winning 57% of the popular vote to Hoover's 39%. It was an historic victory, indeed. Roosevelt's victory was the first since 1848 in which the Democrats won with a majority of the popular vote, and no President from either party had ever won more electoral votes. Furthermore, the Democrats won substantial majorities in the House and Senate. Thereafter, Democrats would hold a majority in the House for all but four years until 1995. It was, without question, precisely the shift the Democrats had hoped it would be.

By the time Roosevelt was inaugurated in March of 1933, the Depression had worsened. Of the 48 states, 32 had closed their banks due to bank runs, and FDR's inauguration came amid the worst bank run in the history of the Depression, which prompted him to act quickly to counter contagion.

Today, of course, one of the things Roosevelt is most remembered for is his first inaugural address, which understandably addressed the pessimistic mood in the nation. Roosevelt began his speech by saying, "I am certain that my fellow Americans expect that on my induction into the Presidency I will address them with a candor and a decision which the present situation of our Nation impels. This is preeminently the time to speak the truth, the whole truth, frankly and boldly. Nor need we shrink from honestly facing conditions in our country today. This great Nation will endure as it has endured, will revive and will prosper. So, first of all, let me assert my firm belief that the only thing we have to fear is fear itself—nameless, unreasoning, unjustified terror which paralyzes needed efforts to convert retreat into advance."

Roosevelt wanted to save the free market system. He feared that the stock market collapse and the onset of the Great Depression, during which 25 percent of the country couldn't find work, could lead to socialism. Indeed, to his left, Senator Huey Long argued for a "share the wealth" program that would redistribute income. To his right, Roosevelt found Republicans largely unwilling to do more than let the economy correct itself.

Thus, the New Deal became a way to regulate the economy rather than take it over. Roosevelt's first 100 Days were unusually active. On his first full day as President, Roosevelt ordered a bank holiday to halt the further run on U.S. banks. He then quickly got to work sending a record number of ideas for bills to Congress, almost all of which were passed easily by the large Democrats majorities in both the House and Senate.

FDR subscribed to a Keynesian view of economics, an outlook that believed the Depression grew worse due to a lack of spending and investment. He thus hoped to stimulate the economy by restoring confidence and offering incentives for people to spend and invest. On March 9th, just four days after Roosevelt declared a bank holiday, Congress passed the Emergency Banking Act, which required all banks to prove they were solvent before they were able to reopen after the bank holiday. FDR hoped this would allow Americans to be confident that their local bank would not lose their money.

From 1933 through 1934, Congress passed the legislation that came to be known as the "First New Deal." New Deal legislation began passing through Congress at the end of March, less than a month into Roosevelt's first term. The first major achievement was the Civilian Conservation Corps (CCC), which put young men between the ages of 18 to 25 to work on a national reforestation program. In mid-April, Roosevelt made an historic move by taking the dollar off the gold standard, thereby giving the Federal Reserve stronger control over the nation's currency.

In May, the Federal Emergency Relief Act was passed, which gave grants rather than loans to states, which allowed them to spend money stimulating their economies. A more controversial act, the Agricultural Adjustment Administration (AAA) passed Congress that same month. The Act paid farmers to NOT till their land, hoping to reduce crop supply, increase prices, and thereby aid ailing farmers in the Heartland.

These initial bills were largely Depression-specific and provided immediate emergency relief. Other bills, however, had a more lasting effect on the economic fabric of the United States. In late May, Congress passed the Federal Securities Act, which required the issuing of stocks and bonds to be registered and approved by the Federal government.

June also brought a flurry of legislative activity. Congress passed the National Industrial Recovery Act (NIRA), the Public Works Administration (PWA), the Farm Credit Act, and the Federal Bank Deposit Insurance Corporation (FDIC), which guaranteed all deposits into insured banks up to a maximum of $2,500. The limit has been increased steadily in each economic crisis since FDR, and was raised to a limit of $250,000 in 2008. Among these pieces of legislation, NIRA was the most controversial. It forced industries to create minimum prices and establish rules of operation within their industry. It also mandated that industries make agreements not to compete. This bill was challenged on legal grounds and would later be found unconstitutional.

Towards the end of 1933, Congress created more Federal jobs programs and ratified the 21st Amendment, ending Prohibition. This was a move heavily favored by Roosevelt's former opponents, the Irish Catholics from the Northeast.

Congress was not finished with the first New Deal in 1933, however. In 1934, it passed the Securities Exchange Act, which established the Securities Exchange Commission (SEC), to clamp down on illegal stock speculation. John F. Kennedy's father, Joseph Kennedy, chaired the Commission. In the same month, Congress passed the Federal Communications Commission (FCC) to regulate radio and telegraphs.

In less than two full years, Franklin Roosevelt achieved more landmark legislative accomplishments than most Presidents had in two terms, but he was still just getting started. The American public was pleased with FDR's actions and awarded him with even larger Democratic majorities in the House and Senate in the 1934 Midterm Elections. However, entering 1935, the First New Deal had only had a small effect on economic recovery: unemployment fell from a high of 25% when Roosevelt was inaugurated to just over 20% by 1935. While it was improvement, the economy was far from bustling again.

In an effort to improve economic conditions, FDR crafted the Second New Deal in an attempt to offer long-term security to the elderly, disabled, unemployed and others in need. The aim of the First New Deal had been merely to stimulate the economy, but the Second New Deal sought to ensure long-term stability.

The Second New Deal was not devoid of stimulus funding, however. One of its first major achievements was the Works Progress Administration (WPA), which employed artists and writers to bring their talents to small towns. More aid was brought to small towns through the Rural Electrification Administration, which brought power to places not served by private companies.

In May of 1935, the Supreme Court dealt FDR's New Deal legislation its first of many defeats when it declared the National Industrial Recovery Act (NIRA) unconstitutional. The following year, it found the Agricultural Adjustment Act unconstitutional as well. During his first term, Roosevelt felt he didn't have a sufficient mandate to take on the court effectively, thus resigning himself to attempting to work around it.

Despite these setbacks, Roosevelt and Congress steamrolled ahead with more major accomplishments. The most important of these were the National Labor Relations Act, the Social Security Act and the Revenue Act.

The Labor Relations Act created the National Labor Relations Board (NLRB), which ensured the right of labor to organize and bargain collectively. This was another piece of legislation influenced heavily by Roosevelt's former opponents in Tammany Hall. The Social Security Act created modern-day Social Security. At the time, it guaranteed a pension for Americans age 65 and over, set up unemployment insurance and assisted states with giving aid to needy citizens, including the disabled.

Apart from reinvigorating the economy, Roosevelt also signed the Neutrality Act in the summer of 1935. The Act prohibited American companies from shipping weapons to belligerents during wartime. Though war had not yet broken out in Europe, Roosevelt's extensive knowledge of the European scene led him to foresee war on the continent.

The New Deal completely revolutionized the relationship between the federal government and its citizens, but FDR's greatest contribution to his country and his party might have come with his wartime leadership. Though America had briefly entered World War I under President Wilson, the nation still believed it was protected by oceans on either side and friendly neighbors to the North and South. Many Americans were content to let Europe fight World War II.

Roosevelt disagreed. During the months and years immediately before the outbreak of war, FDR reiterated America's neutral stance. In May of 1937, another Neutrality Act was passed, now requiring belligerents to pay for non-military U.S. goods in cash and carry them in their own ships. Congress also prohibited the government from loaning money to foreign governments at war. The straw that broke the camel's back, however, was Germany's invasion of Poland in September of 1939. Two days later, France and Great Britain declared war on Germany and World War II began. This event, and those that followed soonafter, changed Roosevelt's mind. As Assistant Secretary of the Navy in World War I, Roosevelt had wanted the U.S. to involve itself earlier. He didn't feel any differently this time around.

Roosevelt knew the time had arrived for America to assert itself on the world stage. A country that large could not pretend to ignore world affairs anymore. He also possessed a keen insight into the dangers of fascism. He knew that Hitler would not stop with the conquest of Europe. America would have to fight the Nazis. And fighting them over there beat fighting them over here.

But how could FDR bring the country along? Famous Americans like Charles Lindbergh were proudly declaring that America should sit out the curent war, and since the Axis had not declared war on America, how could America become involved in the war? Roosevelt initially took small steps. On September 16th, 1940, he signed the Selective Training and Service Act, the first peace-time military draft in US history. All men between the ages of 21 and 35 were required to sign up for the draft.

After winning an unprecedented third term in 1940 – by a significantly smaller, but certainly not narrow, margin than he had previously – Roosevelt began speaking to the American people on the possibility of war in Europe. He framed his arguments in Wilsonian ways, calling the U.S. the last remaining "Arsenal of Democracy." FDR argued that "we are fighting to save a great and precious form of government for ourselves and for the world." He convinced Congress to send aid to Great Britain, on the basis that the US would be defending four essential freedoms. Neutrality was officially over, though war was not yet on.

Roosevelt developed a plan called Lend-Lease. The idea was that the British, who were already at war with Germany, could lease American materials for their wartime effort. When he was asked if this put America in the middle of a war it had not declared, FDR brilliantly deflected the question with an analogy. "Suppose my neighbor's house is burning," he said, "and I have a length of garden hose….I don't say to him…'neighbor my garden hose cost me $15…." The point was not lost on the American people: why not help the Allies fight for themselves? Perhaps the day would never come when America would have to enter the war.

But the with the passage of Lend-Lease by Congress and the acceptance of it by the American people, Roosevelt had transformed American foreign policy. No more would the nation hide behind its borders and not worry about the world; now, America would be willing to actively engage in other parts of the world if only with materials and money. He also established the Democratic Party as an internationalist party while the Republicans tended to be more isolationist.

By the summer of 1941, U.S. entry into the war seemed just on the horizon. Germany violated the Nazi-Soviet Pact and invaded the Soviet Union, spreading war to virtually every piece of the European continent. President Roosevelt and Prime Minister Winston Churchill (another powerful distant relative) met secretly off the coast of Canada in August. The two issued the Atlantic Charter, a statement of Allied goals in the war. It largely reiterated Wilsonian rights, but also specified that a US/UK victory would not lead to territorial expansion or punitive punishment.

However, a substantial segment of the American public did not appreciate the more bellicose direction President Roosevelt seemed to be heading toward. Before the "Greatest Generation" saved Western Europe, many of them were part of the largest anti-war organization in the country's history. In 1940, the United States was still mired in the Great Depression, with nearly 8,000,000 Americans still unemployed, but World War II was the most controversial issue in politics. As the Nazis raced across Western Europe in the first year of the war, young students formed the "America First Committee" in Chicago, an isolationist group supported by future presidents Gerald Ford and John F. Kennedy. The isolationist group aimed to keep the country out of European wars and focus on building America's defenses.

The group expanded to include hundreds of thousands of members by 1941, staunchly opposing President Roosevelt's "Lend-Lease" act, which helped arm the Allies. The America First Committee remained popular and powerful until the morning of December 7, 1941. After the surprise attack by the Japanese, Roosevelt addressed Congress and the nation the following day, giving a stirring speech seeking a declaration of war against Japan. The beginning lines of the speech are instantly familiar, with Roosevelt forever marking Pearl Harbor in the national conscience as "a date which will live in infamy." Of course, the America First Committee instantly became a thing of the past, and the United States began fully mobilizing almost overnight, thanks to the peacetime draft Roosevelt had implemented. The bill helped the country's armed forces swell by two million within months of Pearl Harbor. In 1942 alone, six million men headed off to North Africa, Great Britain and the Pacific Ocean, carrying weapons in one hand and pictures of pin-up models like Betty Grable in the other. Japanese Admiral Hara Tadaichi would later comment, "We won a great tactical victory at Pearl Harbor and thereby lost the war."

Roosevelt signs the declaration of war against Japan

Perhaps FDR's greatest strength as a commander-in-chief lay in his ability to choose great commanders. To oversee wartime operations in Washington, he chose General George Marshall. And to plan and execute the invasion of Europe in 1944, he chose General Dwight D. Eisenhower. After the successful D-Day invasion and the subsequent Allied march across

Europe, FDR began discussing the future of the world with his partners, Winston Churchill of Britain and Josef Stalin of the Soviet Union. It was not FDR's finest hour. In fairness, he was burdened and fatigued by nearly 12 years as president. He also suffered from heart disease and seemed to get weaker and older each day. Still, FDR failed to see the coming Cold War. Churchill suffered no such failure. He lamented that he feared the end of the war would merely exchange the Soviets for the Nazis in Eastern Europe.

Churchill, Roosevelt, and Stalin at Yalta

Roosevelt didn't live to send the end of the war. He died in April 1945 in Warm Springs, Georgia. Vice President Harry Truman, somewhat unprepared for the Presidency, now had to fill some of the biggest shoes in American history. Incredibly, Truman had not been informed of the country's secret attempt to build atomic bombs. Now, faced with the prospect of having to invade Japan and suffering staggering casualties, Truman decided to drop an atomic bomb on Hiroshima on August 6, 1945. When Japan did not surrender, the Americans dropped another atomic bomb on Nagasaki on August 9, 1945. Unbeknownst to the Japanese, the United States had used all the atomic bombs they currently had.

Franklin Delano Roosevelt is frequently ranked among the top three most influential Presidents, and for many historians he vies for the top spot with Abraham Lincoln. Few Presidents face a single crisis on the scale of the Great Depression, but no other President faced dual crises in the way Franklin Roosevelt did.

The First and Second New Deals ushered in landmark legislation that continues to have an impact on the American economy. Most importantly, the Social Security Act, the Federal Deposit Insurance Corporation, the Securities and Exchange Commission and the Federal Communications Commission all continue to affect the fabric of American life and the nation's political debates. Other domestic legislation of a more temporary nature left an enduring impression on American society. Among these, the GI Bill allowed for the continued expansion of the US economy and the growth of the all-American suburb. Millions of Americans were catapulted into the middle class because of their service to the country in World War II. On the economy, Roosevelt's presidency was an enormous success, ending the Great Depression, and bringing unemployment from a high of 25% when he entered office to a low of less than 2% when he left. The nation went from bust to boom in just over 12 years.

On foreign policy, Roosevelt mobilized Americans effectively and won World War II, though not without some defeats along the way. Roosevelt's enormous popularity helped him to mobilize the nation in support of war, and prepared the nation for the later attack on Pearl Harbor.

Roosevelt's legacy is not without critics, however. Because Roosevelt's enormous expansion of the Federal Government is still hotly debated today, FDR is assessed differently by partisans. With the Great Recession of 2008, President Obama looked to the FDR legacy as a guide. Republicans and conservatives suggested he look elsewhere. Some historians and their GOP allies contend that the American economy did not recover because of the New Deal, but only because of the massive industrial build-up brought by the US' entry into World War II. Critics point to the "Depression within a Depression" that occurred in 1938, when unemployment actually increased from about 14% to 19% within a year. Unemployment was never able to get below 14% until 1941, when the U.S. entered the war, at which point unemployment rapidly declined much faster than it had in Roosevelt's first two terms in office, down to less than 2% by 1945.

Even on foreign policy, Roosevelt's legacy is not immune from criticism. The impending Cold War becomes crucial to assessing Roosevelt's legacy. Was Roosevelt strong enough in opposing Soviet expansion into Eastern Europe and Asia? Some view Roosevelt's concessions to the Soviets at the final Yalta Conference as horribly unwise. The US was winning the war in Japan, and with the British freed up by an impending victory in Europe, it wasn't clear that the Soviets were needed all that much. The Manhattan Project was progressing steadily, and the U.S. would soon have a nuclear bomb. Perhaps FDR could have limited the Soviets more effectively.

Regardless of these criticisms, there is no doubt that Franklin Roosevelt's lengthy Presidency was one of the most transformative in history, for better or for worse. The size and role of the Federal Government took on its greatest expansion in history, and became responsible for ensuring basic minimum economic guarantees to its citizens. With the end of World War II, the

US was positioned as the world's most viable super power, with the Soviet Union a rapidly expanding second. The collapse of the British Empire ensured that the US would replace it as the leader of the Western free world. The United States we know today – the most powerful nation in the world – owes its origins almost directly to Franklin Roosevelt, whose political courage on the New Deal and support for military mobilization, coupled with his enormous popularity, ensured that the U.S. was well positioned to lead the world anew.

Chapter 7: Forging a New Path

Harry Truman represented a polar opposite to FDR in many ways. He was a Southerner and he was a self-made man; where FDR was charming and glib, Truman was gruff and profane. As discussions commenced in the White House about the looming Japanese surrender, someone suggested it be done in a way that protected Japan's honor. "They lost their honor at Pearl Harbor," Truman snarled.

Wars often produce unintended consequences, and so it proved to be with World War II. One of the most dramatic changes produced by the war came on the issue that had haunted the country (and the Democratic Party) from the outset: race. As the party of states' rights, the Democrats had always struggled with how to deal with minorities. Jefferson said he "trembled" when he reflected on God being just, yet he sipped wine while his slaves built Monticello. This contradiction had defined the Democratic Party for generations.

World War II had just made racism even more inconvenient. During the Battle of the Bulge, General Eisenhower needed more troops at the front. He went against War Department guidelines and invited African-American infantry troops (who usually served in support roles) to serve at the front next to white soldiers. The order didn't take effect until later in the war, but the African-American troops performed well. Additionally, the success of the Tuskegee Airman had not gone unnoticed by the American people. These were African-American pilots who saw combat action first by escorting heavy bombers and later in dive-bombing and strafing missions.

While the suffrage movement for women eventually obtained the right to vote for women when the 19th Amendment was ratified in 1920, Jim Crow laws throughout the South continued to reduce blacks to second class citizens. Still, it's important to recall that the South was not the only region where segregation was the flavor of the era. In much of the North, African Americans regularly were denied the right to vote, impeded from jury service (causing injury both to the defendant and to the prospective juror and sometimes to the State as well), and excluded from public places like theaters, restaurants, hotels, and inns. Still, in most Northern states African Americans could vote and send their children to decent public schools, though obviously they still encountered discrimination in housing and jobs — both public and private ones. From 1910-1970, a cumulative seven million African Americans left the South, in what became known as the *Great Migration*.

During the presidency of President Woodrow Wilson, which was best remembered for World War I and his foreign policy goals, the federal government started to follow some segregation policies.[1] Wilson's government required segregation in federal buildings; African American employees' desks were curtained off from those of white employees's desks; separate bathrooms and separate lunch-time tables were arranged. When Wilson's segregationist policies were challenged, Wilson defended them with the argument that segregation was "'not humiliating, but a benefit,'" and that Wilson's policies were "'rendering [the Negroes] more safe in their possession of office, and less likely to be discriminated against.'"[2]

This government-required segregation of the races continued into the middle of the 20th century. In World War I and World War II, African Americans predominantly were required to serve in separate military units. In 1948, President Harry S Truman, as commander in chief, ordered that American service personnel were no longer to be segregated. Truman was led in this decision by the realization that American segregation, notably in the military (the Nation's most public and prominent institution), was inadvertently helping the Soviet Union's propaganda. That was intolerable to an American Presidency which was committed to rebuilding post-war Europe's Western democracies through the Marshall Plan, so that the shadow of Soviet Communism would not dominate Western Europe.

With that, the Civil Rights Movement began to gain new momentum. In the courts, bright young lawyers like Thurgood Marshall began filing cases to overturn segregation in schools. The ultimate successes of the Civil Rights Movement can be explained by the fact that those Court decisions were not part of just the litigation strategy; they were supplemented, heavily, by civic education, political efforts and lobbying in government halls, and labor organizing. At the forefront of many of these efforts was the National Association for the Advancement of Colored People (NAACP), founded in 1909. The NAACP sought hard to close the curtain on racial discrimination through these means. *Brown*, which rejected the "separate but equal" doctrine, was its crown jewel, but *Brown* was also instrumental in starting the second phase of the Movement. *Brown* understood that the disparity engendered by discrimination was more than just a disparity in the financing of facilities: "To separate [African American children] from others of similar age and qualifications solely because of their race generates a feeling of inferiority as to their status in the community that may affect their hearts and minds in a way

---

[1] 110 Cong. Rec. 6543-6544 (1964) (remarks of Sen. Humphrey) ("Large sums of money are contributed by the United States each year for the construction, operation, and maintenance of segregated schools. Similarly, under the Hill-Burton Act, Federal grants are made to hospitals which admit whites only or Negroes only. . . . In higher education also, a substantial part of the Federal grants to colleges, medical schools and so forth, in the South is still going to segregated institutions. Nor is this all. In several States, agricultural extension services, supported by Federal funds, maintain racially segregated offices for Negroes and whites. . . . Vocational training courses, supported with Federal funds, are given in segregated schools and institutions and often limit Negroes to training in less skilled occupations. In particular localities it is reported that Negroes have been cut off from relief rolls, or denied surplus agricultural commodities, or otherwise deprived of the benefit of federally assisted programs, in retaliation for their participation in voter registration drives, sit-in demonstrations and the like.").

[2] R. Kluger, SIMPLE JUSTICE, *supra*, at 91.

unlikely ever to be undone."[3] From today's vantage point, it is difficult to understand the kind of resistance *Brown* engendered since "the idea of *Brown* remains largely sacred in American political culture."[4] In that sense, *Brown* was an end as well as a means.

Meanwhile, the Democratic Party threatened to rip apart at the seams over issue. The same issue that had elected Lincoln—the division of Northern liberals from Southern conservatives in the Democratic Party—now threatened to end the Truman presidency. To his credit, Truman decided to take the issue head on. In 1948, he issued an executive order desegregating the Army. It was perhaps his greatest moment as president; and one that dramatically changed the Democratic Party by finally giving it a chance to win African-American votes.

Truman then set out on an old-fashioned "whistle-stop" tour in a train and campaigned around the country. He ran a tough race and won a surprising victory in November 1948. As he prepared to begin to serve his own term as president, Truman presided over a very different party than the one first created by Thomas Jefferson. The party still said it stood for states' rights and limited government, but more and more it was finding ways to use government to help working people, even minorities. And now America was a major player on the international stage. By 1949, the Democratic Party was the internationalist party.

It was a new world, a new country and a new party. But the changes were just beginning.

Chapter 8: A New Frontier

After his 1948 election, Truman continued to pursue the policies of this new party. One of the best examples of this was found in his concern that Europe be rebuilt so as not to allow another war to stop. The result was the Marshall Plan, where vast sums of American money were spent to rebuild the economies of Europe and prevent the spread of Soviet communism. Closer to home, he continued to expand government in ways that were designed to help the working class. He became the first president to call for nationalized health insurance.

When North Korea attacked South Korea in 1950, Truman again found himself as a wartime president. When his commander, General Douglas MacArthur, publically argued with the

---

[3] 347 U.S., at 494.
[4] J. Balkin et al., WHAT *BROWN V. BOARD OF EDUCATION* SHOULD HAVE SAID: THE NATION'S TOP LEGAL EXPERTS REWRITE AMERICA'S LANDMARK CIVIL RIGHTS DECISION 4 (NYU Press, 2002) ("It was not always thus. . . . Even many defenders of the result had little good to say about the opinion, arguing that its overruling of previous precedents was abrupt and unexplained and that its use of social science to demonstrate the harm that segregation imposed on black children was unconvincing. The day after the decision, May 18, 1954, James Reston wrote in the New York Times that the Court had rejected 'history, philosophy, and custom' in basing its decision in 'the primacy of the general welfare. . . . Relying more on the social scientists than on legal precedents – a procedure often in controversy in the past -- the Court insisted on equality of the mind and heart rather than on equal school facilities. . . . The Court's opinion read more like an expert paper on sociology than a Supreme Court opinion.' If the defenders of Brown were uneasy, its opponents were positively incensed by the decision. People who accuse the contemporary Supreme Court of abusing its office may forget how deeply *Brown* was resented, especially in the South.").

president about battle strategy, Truman fired him. The decision was roundly criticized at the time; but over the years, history has vindicated Truman's defense of civilian control over the military as the right call. Still, his popularity plummeted and he watched in vain as Adlai Stevenson, the Democratic candidate for president in 1952, failed to beat Republican Dwight Eisenhower.

By then, the Democratic Party had transformed itself and overcome decades of being in the minority following the Civil War. The Roosevelt-Truman administrations had once again made the Democratic Party the majority party in America. The coalition that had been assembled was deep and wide: unions, intellectuals, farmers, Southerners, urbanites and increasingly (thanks to Harry Truman) racial minorities. Prior to FDR, the Democrats' relationship with many of these groups had been tenuous at best. Many minorities and women had previously seen the Democratic Party as the party of the South, of segregation and of a society dominated by white males. Now, a new more durable Democratic coalition had emerged.

Perhaps the greatest evidence of the strength and durability of this new Democratic coalition could be found in the Eisenhower administration. Ike served as a Republican president, but after five consecutive Democratic victories in the presidential race, it was inevitable Republicans would eventually win again. Yet President Eisenhower possessed a shrewd political mind and he did little to overturn the reforms of the New Deal years. In some ways, Eisenhower embraced these reforms. He invested tax dollars in school construction and a new interstate highway system. The Eisenhower administration consolidated the New Deal's gains, and it reinforced Truman's "containment" strategy, a foreign policy vis-à-vis the Soviet Union that would become bipartisan for decades.

In the 1960 election, the Democrats chose John F. Kennedy as their nominee. Kennedy came from a privileged background but had a gift for politics. Handsome and charismatic, his name had first appeared on the national stage during the 1956 Democratic convention when he was briefly considered as Adlai Stevenson's running mate. During the 1960 campaign, he continued in the internationalist vein of FDR and Truman and even took it up a notch in sharply criticizing the Eisenhower administration for a supposed "missile gap" with the Soviets. Kennedy presented himself as war veteran who would stand vigilant in the Cold War with the Soviet Union.

He also sensed an opportunity to expand the New Deal coalition. Though many African-Americans had begun to vote Democratic after 1948, Eisenhower and the Republicans still received a healthy number of African-American votes in 1952 and 1956. When civil rights leader Martin Luther King was unjustly imprisoned in 1960, Kennedy decided to place a phone call to King's wife, Coretta, expressing his sympathy. The move was heralded throughout the black community and marked a key turning point in the African-American migration to the Democratic Party. Though King himself stayed officially neutral, his father, Martin Luther King, Sr, endorsed Kennedy even though he expressed reservations about the candidate's Catholicism. When he heard about it, Kennedy responded with characteristic humor that he was surprised to learn King's father held bigoted views. "We all have fathers," he joked to an aide, a reference to his own dad's shady past.

Once in office, Kennedy set about to create what he called "the New Frontier." This was yet another expansion of the safety net policies that Democrats had begun to push for under Woodrow Wilson. Kennedy pushed for legislation to help with housing and farming. He also pushed for increases in Social Security. Perhaps most importantly for the Democratic Party, he made the party the champion of space exploration. He challenged the country to put a man on the moon by the end of the 1960s and he pushed for funding for NASA.

On the world stage, Kennedy continued the internationalist policies of Roosevelt and Truman. He inherited a limited military engagement in Vietnam and increased the American presence there. His theory was that America had a role to play in holding back the tide of communist expansion. At the time, most of the country seemed to agree with the strategy.

Perhaps the most vexing challenge Kennedy faced came on civil rights. His 1960 phone call to Mrs. King had been meaningful to African-Americans; but it was largely symbolic. While the bulk of Kennedy's legacy deals with foreign policy, significant domestic upheavals were occurring in the United States during his Presidency. Most important among these was the Civil

Rights Movement.

Kennedy's record on civil rights is mixed. In the House and Senate, he often sided with conservative Southern Democrats. And though he ran for President in favor of civil rights, he didn't believe his narrow victory gave him a mandate for decisive action on the issue. For most of 1961 and part of 1962, Kennedy essentially made no movement on civil rights, despite the spread of protest and action, led by Martin Luther King, throughout the South.

Nevertheless, Kennedy and his brother Robert often found themselves forced into action by conflict between authorities and minorities and protesters in the South. After ensuring Meredith's attendance in 1962, a similar situation broke out in 1963, when Alabama's Governor George Wallace personally prevented two African-American students from enrolling in the University of Alabama. Again, Kennedy sent in federal troops against the state's Governor.

In between these events, Kennedy had proposed a limited civil rights act that focused primarily on voting rights, but it avoided more controversial topics of equal employment and desegregation. Kennedy was toeing the line between maintaining political support in the South while also holding liberal Democrats. Until the end of his Presidency, however, a coalition of Southern Democrats and Republicans prevented any action on the bill, and Kennedy was never able to sign it into law.

Apart from civil rights, Kennedy made some headway on other domestic policy issues. He successfully passed an increase of the minimum wage and aid to public schools. Otherwise, though, most of Kennedy's New Frontier proposals failed to pass through Congress, including his Medicare bill. It would fall upon his successor, Lyndon Johnson, who had spent the 1950s mastering Senate parliamentarianism, to enact much of the New Frontier in the form of the Great Society. And it would be Johnson who pushed forth more stringent protections on civil rights than Kennedy had ever proposed.

Kennedy sympathized with the civil rights movement but had to balance that sympathy with the large number of Southern Democrats in his coalition who still clung to the Jeffersonian notion of states' rights. Dr. King himself became impatient with Kennedy's inaction on civil rights legislation and staged events in the South designed to provoke police and generate pressure on Kennedy. It worked. When Bull Connor unleashed fire hoses and dogs on peaceful demonstrators in Birmingham in 1963, the nation was outraged. So was the president. In a nationally televised address, he called for major civil rights legislation. Later that summer, Kenned welcomed Dr. King to the White House following the minister's stirring address in front of the Lincoln Memorial. "I have a dream, too," he said as he shook Dr. King's hand.

Sadly, Kennedy wouldn't live to see the dream come true. In November 1963, an assassin in Dallas killed him. While the nation mourned, a new president took the oath of office aboard Air Force I. His administration would take the Democratic Party to new heights…as well as new lows.

Americans today consistently rank President Kennedy among the greatest Presidents in the nation's history. Academics, however, are not quite as eager to carve Kennedy into Mount Rushmore. Few Presidents face such a large disparity between their historical memory and the actual facts of their Presidencies. Kennedy's assassination – the first ever to be captured on video through the Zapruder Film – has caused Americans to selectively remember Kennedy through the prism of his assassination.

While President Kennedy was a generally popular President, at the point of his assassination roughly 55% of the country approved of the job he was doing. While not bad, that number is hardly historic: a 55% approval rating was about the average for most Presidents during normal times after Kennedy left office. More importantly, Kennedy was in Texas due to worries about reelection. Despite this, Americans view President Kennedy as one of the nation's most influential and inspiring, and have done so since very shortly after his death.

The country seems to be suffering from a sort of collective amnesia. Reviewing the Kennedy Presidency in terms of its tangible accomplishments leaves much to be desired. After all, Kennedy's Presidency was one of the shortest in history, at less than three years in total.

On foreign policy, President Kennedy's first year and a half in office was not only unproductive, but outright disastrous. Botching the Bay of Pigs invasion had devastating results in the later Cuban Missile Crisis. Not until 1963 are the US and USSR able to agree on a nuclear testing treaty, and a nimble one at that. The war Americans want to forget – the Vietnam War – began on Kennedy's watch, though Kennedy warned against further escalation, advice his successor did heed.

Without question the most successful foreign policy moment for President Kennedy came with his successful negotiation of the Cuban Missile Crisis. For this, he is rightly remembered fondly for avoiding nuclear war. On the other hand, would the Cuban Missile Crisis have happened were it not for Kennedy's failure with the Bay of Pigs? Arguably not. When the Bay of Pigs failed, the Soviets saw a weak American President unwilling to follow through on failures with Cuba, and so they saw an opening to station missiles in Cuba. Only because of Kennedy's failure did he have a chance to succeed.

On domestic policy, Kennedy only achieved negligible parts of his New Frontier policy. On the civil rights issue, he was timid, only coming around to mild concessions for African-Americans in the later months of his Presidency. Martin Luther King's March on Washington was partly a protest against Kennedy's limited proposal, and in favor of a stronger bill.

When Kennedy was assassinated on November 22nd, 1963, however, his death may have actually given his successor the necessary mandate to achieve the New Frontier – and then some

– that Kennedy was unable to. Johnson defeated Barry Goldwater with over 60% of the popular vote in 1964, giving him a decisive mandate to govern. Johnson's more "down home" character arguably allowed him to appeal more broadly to Americans than John Kennedy's reelection might have. Most importantly, Johnson's relations with Congress were infinitely better than Kennedy's. On domestic policy, Kennedy achieved little beyond the Peace Corps, which was an executive order issued independent of Congress. Johnson, however, pushed groundbreaking legislation through Congress using his deep legislative knowledge. This included Medicare, a program originally proposed by President Kennedy.

Chapter 9: The Great Society

LBJ

Lyndon Baines Johnson hailed from Johnson City, Texas. Tall and imposing, he had a habit of putting his hands on people as he talked to them, and he was nothing if not a political genius. One of his biographers has referred to him as the "Master of the Senate" during his time as Senate Majority Leader. He often said he knew what power was, he knew where to find it and he knew how to use it.

In November 1963, when Vice President Johnson became President of the United States, he had finally reached the top of what Disraeli called the "greasy poll." From the start, his political skill could be seen.

It began with civil rights. As a Southern senator, Johnson had never been a leader on the issue; indeed, in many ways he had sided with segregationists like his friend and mentor Senator Richard Russell of Georgia. Moreover, Kennedy had picked him as a vice presidential candidate in order to appeal to the conservative Democrats of the South who were weary of a Northeastern

Irish Catholic Democrat.

However, once he became president, LBJ saw a golden opportunity to finish the job Lincoln had begun of liberating African-Americans. He also foresaw that civil rights would lead to an influx of minority voters into the Democratic Party even if it meant losing Southern whites to the Republican Party.

As it turned out, it would be Johnson that passed the crown jewel of the Civil Rights Movement.[5] On July 2, 1964, President Johnson signed into law the National Civil Rights Act of 1964, which banned discrimination based on "race, color, religion, or national origin" in employment practices and public accommodations. Indeed, the Civil Rights Act of 1964 could not have passed without the support of President Lyndon B. Johnson, whose background as a white southern Democrat made him an unlikely supporter of civil rights. However, other white southerners in Congress, all Democrats, opposed the bill, and attempted to prevent its passage through the Senate by a never-ending debate on the bill, known as a filibuster. The filibuster failed, largely due to President Johnson's significant arm-twisting skills.

This time, instead of the Supreme Court being unable to enforce its opinion, Congress had the powers to enforce the Civil Rights Act. Though the legislation's stated powers of enforcement were weak, Congress used the Commerce Clause in Article I of the Constitution to enforce provisions such as ending segregation practices in hotels (because blacks might be traveling across state lines to stay in a hotel, for example). Congress also used the Equal Protection Clause of the Fourteenth Amendment to assert its authority.

When asked by a civil rights leader why he had changed and become a champion of civil rights, Johnson reflected on his ascension to the Oval Office and how this had liberated him from being a parochial senator from Texas. "Free at last, free at last, thank God Almighty, I'm free at last," he said in quoting Martin Luther King. In 1965, Johnson also signed legislation changing the immigration patterns to the U.S., thus accelerating the racial diversity in America.

Johnson saw civil rights as part of a larger plan for America that he called "the Great Society." Again, like Wilson, FDR, Truman and Kennedy, he wanted to use government to help people live their lives. And for Johnson, there seemed no limits to the good government could do. He created the Head Start program for early education; he created the "war on poverty" to greatly increase funding for the impoverished; and he created Medicare and Medicaid to help provide health care to the elderly and the poor, respectively.

In 1965, Johnson signed the Voting Rights Act of 1965,[6] which restored and secured voting

---

[5] 78 Stat. 252, as amended, 42 U.S.C. § 2000d *et seq*. This Act gives the Executive Branch power to end federal funding of private programs that use race as a means of disadvantaging racial minorities in any manner that would be forbidden by the Constitution were the *government* to conduct it.

[6] 42 U.S.C. §§ 1973 *et seq*.

rights for all Americans, as well as the Immigration and Nationality Services Act of 1965,[7] which had less to do with then-citizens and more to do with potential future citizens and which substantially lessened the barrier to United States entry to non-European immigrants. Finally, Johnson signed the Fair Housing Act of 1968,[8] which forbade discrimination in the sale or rental of accommodation.

President Johnson and King after signing the Voting Rights Act of 1965

Collectively these laws became known as Lyndon Johnson's *Great Society Program.* Another component of this program was Johnson's nomination of Justice Thurgood Marshall, the NAACP's chief advocate in *Brown* and other cases, to the United States Supreme Court.[9] Along with the Vietnam War that Johnson would be accused of escalating, the *Great Society Program* was deemed to be the reason that many, including Johnson himself, believed led to Johnson's unpopularity and his eventual decision in 1968 not to seek the Democratic Party's re-nomination

---

[7] Pub.L. 89-236; 79 Stat. 911.
[8] Pub.L. 90-284, 82 Stat. 73. C. Lamb & E. Wilk, *Civil Rights, Federalism, and the Administrative Process: Favorable Outcomes by Federal, State, and Local Agencies in Housing Discrimination Complaints*, Public Administration Review 418 (May/June 2010) ("the federal government's enforcement of national policy does not necessarily lead to the most favorable administrative outcomes for complainants — even in civil rights, where state and local governments have had poor records in the past.").
[9] Justice Marshall, of course, has been cited in this very essay with some frequency.

for the Presidency of the United States.

Perhaps the most overlooked legislative provision -- as part of the 1964 Civil Rights Act – came after President John F. Kennedy's term (during President Lyndon B. Johnson) and upon President Kennedy's exhortation: 42 U.S.C. § 2000d (tying federal funds to non-discrimination).[10] In requiring that programs that receive federal moneys end racial discrimination, by and large Congress has free rein.[11] There is evidence in the congressional record that such evidence was being documented.[12] In greater numbers, African Americans re-entered politics in the South, and across the country young people were inspired to action. Through this period, the Supreme Court did uphold these federal laws as consistent with Congress's interstate commerce powers as well as its authority "to enforce by appropriate legislation" the Civil War Amendments.[13] It is doubtful whether that would have happened in today's climate, given the present Supreme Court's reluctance to readily embrace the congressional commerce power since the mid-1990's.[14]

Two other factors that may have helped make significant inroads were changing social attitudes due to stifling worldview of the 1950's and the Vietnam War. The War probably made Americans realize the necessity to give African Americans equal citizenship stature and also America's renewed need, just like during the *Brown* era against the Soviet Union, to show its in-house *equality* to guard against the North Vietnamese Communists's propaganda accentuating American *inequality*.

---

[10] "No person in the United States shall, on the ground of race, color, or national origin, be excluded from participation in, be denied the benefits of, or be subjected to discrimination under any program or activity receiving Federal financial assistance."

[11] *South Dakota v. Dole*, 483 U.S. 203 (1987) (articulating that even though Congress's spending power authority is broad, it faces four limitations: (i) "the exercise of the spending power must be in pursuit of 'the general welfare'"; (ii) "if Congress desires to condition the States' receipt of federal funds, it 'must do so unambiguously . . . , enabl[ing] the States to exercise their choice knowingly, cognizant of the consequences of their participation'"; (iii) "conditions on federal grants might be illegitimate if they are unrelated 'to the federal interest in particular national projects or programs'"; and (iv) "other constitutional provisions may provide an independent bar to the conditional grant of federal funds.").

[12] 110 Cong. Rec. 1519 (1964) (statement of Congressman E. Celler, Chairman of the House Judiciary Committee) ("The bill would offer assurance that hospitals financed by Federal money would not deny adequate care to Negroes. It would prevent abuse of food distribution programs whereby Negroes have been known to be denied food surplus supplies when white persons were given such food. It would assure Negroes the benefits now accorded only white students in programs of high[er] education financed by Federal funds. It would, in short, assure the existing right to equal treatment in the enjoyment of Federal funds. It would not destroy any rights of private property or freedom of association."); *id.*, at 2467 ("In general, it seems rather anomalous that the Federal Government should aid and abet discrimination on the basis of race, color, or national origin by granting money and other kinds of financial aid. It seems rather shocking, moreover, that, while we have on the one hand the 14th Amendment, which is supposed to do away with discrimination, since it provides for equal protection of the laws, on the other hand, we have the Federal Government aiding and abetting those who persist in practicing racial discrimination.").

[13] *Katzenbach v. Morgan*, 384 U.S. 641 (1966); *South Carolina v. Katzenbach*, 383 U.S. 301 (1966); *Heart of Atlanta Motel, Inc. v. United States*, 379 U.S. 241 (1964); *Katzenbach v. McClung*, 379 U.S. 294 (1964).

[14] See, *e.g., United States v. Lopez,* 514 U.S. 549 (1995).

Yet Johnson's domestic policy achievements were soon overshadowed by his decision to expand the war in Vietnam. Johnson sent hundreds of thousands of troops to Southeast Asia in an attempt to fight and win what he called "that bitch of a war." He desperately wanted to focus his time and attention on the Great Society at home, but he increasingly found himself overwhelmed by events in Vietnam. Strategically, Johnson faced a unique challenge: America was fighting a traditional war while the Vietnamese communists were fighting a guerilla war. As a result, American troops never lost a battle…but never could vanquish their opponent.

Although hundreds of thousands protested the war in 1967, including Martin Luther King, Jr., a majority of the public still supported it, due in large part to the Johnson's administration public confidence. But as General Westmoreland talked of victory at the end of 1967, the Viet Cong launched a massive assault across South Vietnam in January 1968. Known as the Tet Offensive, the Viet Cong suffered hundreds of thousands of casualties, and the American forces never lost a battle. But American support for the war still plummeted.

By 1968, with mounting casualties and increasingly bad press coverage of the war, public opposition to the war had grown. This perhaps surprised the normally politically-astute LBJ. He saw his Vietnam policy as a continuation of the Democratic Party's position of fighting the Cold War and stopping communist expansion. Hadn't John F. Kennedy promised the United States would "bear any burden" in his inaugural address?

The Tet Offensive made President Johnson non-credible and historically unpopular, and he did not run for reelection in 1968. By then, Vietnam had already fueled the hippie counterculture, and anti-war protests spread across the country. On campuses and in the streets, some protesters spread peace and love, but others rioted. In August 1968, riots broke out in the streets of Chicago, as the National Guard and police took on 10,000 anti-war rioters during the Democratic National Convention. Johnson left office a destroyed man. In many ways, his party had been diminished, too.

Following the 1968 election, the Democratic Party entered a wilderness period that was punctuated only by a brief and unsuccessful term for Jimmy Carter and would last until 1992. Carter's unhappy four years still provided some important seed-planting for the future. Though most Americans remember the Carter years for inflation and hostages, the peanut farmer proved to be a surprisingly conservative president. He de-regulated the airline industry, began the process of decontrolling oil prices and dramatically increased defense spending in 1980 in response to Soviet aggression in Afghanistan. Still, the 1980 election saw the launch of the Reagan Revolution. The governing coalition carefully pieced together by FDR and Truman had frayed and come apart. Fortunately for Democrats, a new leader would emerge who understood the history of the party as well as the failures of the Great Society. His mission was to invent a new brand that he called "New Democrats."

Chapter 10: The New Democrats

William Jefferson Clinton was a natural. As a boy, he had met John F. Kennedy. As a college student, he had worked for Senator William Fulbright as he challenged the Johnson administration over Vietnam. And as a young governor of Arkansas, he had learned how to weave together a Democratic philosophy that could still win votes in conservative Arkansas. In some ways he resembled that other Southern governor who became president—Jimmy Carter. Like Carter, Clinton believed that the party needed to offer a moderate if not conservative domestic agenda. But unlike Carter, Clinton possessed a dazzling charm and personality that drew people to him and to his policies.

Governor Clinton and President Carter, 1978

As governor of Arkansas in the 1980s, Clinton also maintained a national profile as a prominent voice and leader among the Third Way New Democrats. This group maintained a tricky balance with the Democratic National Committee and the more liberal wing of the Democratic Party, which included liberal stalwart and "Lion of the Senate", Ted Kennedy of Massachusetts, the Kennedy scion. The New Democrats, officially organized as the Democratic Leadership Council (DLC), were kind of a renegade or rogue branch of the Democratic Party that called for welfare reform and smaller government, which was popular among much of the political spectrum save for those on the far left.

Despite the political differences within the Democratic Party, politicians like Clinton realized they would always have the support and votes of the far left simply because the Republicans would always be anathema. Moreover, as the New Democrats seemed to represent more mainstream positions, other members of the liberal establishment had to acknowledge, even if grudgingly, that Clinton and politicians of that ilk may be viewed in a better light. To that end, Clinton was asked to deliver the Democratic Party response to the immensely popular President Ronald Reagan's 1985 State of the Union Address and served as Chair of the National Governors Association from 1986 to 1987.

All of this gave Clinton, who was still only in his late 30's, enormous exposure. Clinton positioned himself astutely by avoiding ideological battles of prior liberal eras and instead making his priorities economic expansion, job creation and educational reforms. To help senior citizens and thus invoke the Great Society as well as Franklin Delano Roosevelt's New Deal, Clinton got rid of the sales tax attending medications and expanded the home property-tax exemption.

Clinton had studied history and viewed LBJ as a great but flawed man. He also understood the backlash to the spending of the Great Society that culminated in the Reagan years. It's important to note that Clinton served as Governor of Arkansas during the time that Reagan served as president. He saw Reagan's popularity as he presented a Republican philosophy that offered a strong national defense and a growing economy helped by tax cuts.

In 1992, Clinton ran for president as a conservative Democrat. He called for a middle class tax cut; he called for a strong national defense; and perhaps most famously, he called for an "end to welfare as we know it." This last campaign promise sent a signal to America that Clinton would be a different kind of Democrat. After all, who had given the American people welfare as they knew it? Democrats in general, and LBJ specifically. Thus, in one masterstroke, Clinton was able to separate himself from what they didn't like about the modern Democratic Party while showing he shared the Democratic policies that people did like.

During the summer of 1992, Clinton took the lead over Bush for a variety of reasons. At the core, Clinton struck a stark contrast to Bush by appearing as a much fresher face and simply a smoother politician. While Clinton appeared on MTV and famously played the saxophone on the Arsenio Hall Show, Bush shot himself in the foot by expressing amazement at the way a supermarket could scan codes at the checkout aisle. The debates also put the contrast on display. Clinton connected with voters in town hall formats in a way few politicians ever could, while Bush was criticized for looking at his watch to check the time during a debate. And by putting the first President Bush on the spot by asking him the price of milk during a public debate (an answer that Bush did not at the time know), Clinton was able to make himself look like the "the People's Candidate" as opposed to the more elite and out-of-touch Bush.

President George H.W. Bush

As president, Clinton initially tacked to the left and pushed for national health care. The core element of the plan was requiring employers to provide health insurance for their employees. Dating back to World War II when wages were capped, employers had begun offering health insurance as another way of compensating employees. Since that time, America's health care increasingly had been provided at the office, but not all businesses offered health insurance, and employees without it had to fend for themselves and pay exorbitant rates.

Clinton hoped this mandate would solve that problem and appeal to middle class voters, but it didn't. A huge backlash ensued as television ads paid for by business groups warned Americans that these reforms would dramatically harm health care. As shrewd as the Clintons generally are, they forgot four critical considerations: (*i*) State healthcare raises far fewer eyebrows than federal healthcare (larger territory, more diverse, much more contentious to establish, let alone manage); (*ii*) the Clintons were playing a greater stakes roulette and their enemies who hated them vehemently would stop at nothing to derail this item and thus to exact revenge or preclude work on *other* issues (many opponents had nothing to do with health care; they simply saw an Achilles heel they sensed was vulnerable); (*iii*) urban healthcare is not the same as general healthcare which people frequently see as intrusive and incursive of their personal liberty to make healthcare and HMO decisions; and finally, (*iv*) only the Clintons (particularly Bill) had found the whole "two for the price of one" tagline or even notion even remotely humorous or acceptable. Most people, out of sexism or a sense of the proper province of the Presidential spouse, thought the First Lady should stick to being White House hostess and a mute but smiling goodwill ambassador for the country. That was the traditional role that almost every First Lady, save for Edith Wilson (wife of President Woodrow Wilson) during the incapacitated days of President Wilson, had played up until that point. Voters too generally believed that their votes had been cast for *Bill*, not *Hillary*.

Over 15 years later, many political experts and pundits predicted the Obama Administration's push for healthcare was rather a losing effort like the Clinton Administration's had been. But Obama had never fully invested in the public option or the single-payer mechanism which seems to have been the Clinton Administration's almost non-negotiable starting point in 1993. When even a compromise legislative effort by the Senate majority leader Democrat George Mitchell of Maine failed in August 1993, it was clear that the reform was not going to pass then. And moreover Obama spent almost *all* of his political capital of his first few years in office on healthcare.[15] Clinton had not. Universal healthcare reform was the legislation that doomed the first few years of the Clinton Administration and caused significant losses of Democratic seats in both houses of Congress. Clinton would famously take the message from the midterm elections and announce in his 1996 State of the Union Address, "The era of big government is over". Though that is one of Clinton's most memorable soundbytes, the followup to that statement is often left out. Clinton continued, "[B]ut we cannot go back to the time when our citizens were left to fend for themselves. We must go forward as one America, one nation working together, to meet the challenges we face together. Self-reliance and teamwork are not opposing virtues -- we must have both."

Nevertheless, Clinton was not deterred. Clinton fought hard for and was able to sign into law the Brady Bill (so named after the secret service protection of President Ronald Reagan who was paralyzed by a gunman's bullet intended to maim and/or kill Reagan) on November 30, 1993. This statute imposed a five-day waiting period on handgun purchases throughout the United States. President Clinton also was able to expand the Earned Income Tax Credit, which essentially was a subsidy for low-income workers, and Clinton refused to flinch in the absence of

---

[15] There is a certain symmetry or coming full circle in the Clinton-Obama saga. It is also clear that the Obama Administration's domestic policy achievements in its first few years would have been close to nil had the United States Supreme Court nullified the Patient Protection and Affordable Care Act (PPACA), so insistently passed by the Obama Administration. Chief Justice John Roberts's controlling opinion in *National Federation of Independent Business v. Sebelius*, 2012 U.S. Lexis 4876, * (2012), upholding the crux (the individual mandate, requiring most persons in the United States to purchase health insurance or pay a penalty) of the PPACA. While Chief Justice Roberts rejected the more expected twin justifications, the Commerce Clause, U.S. Const. art. I, § 8, cl. 3, and the Necessary and Proper Clause, U.S. Const. art. I, § 8, cl. 18, thus jeopardizing a future course of Congressional action, he did form a majority with Justices Ginsburg, Breyer, Sotomayor and Kagan to uphold the mandate as an exercise of Congress's taxing power under the Constitution. Chief Justice Roberts, joined by Justices Breyer and Kagan, and with the combined votes of Justices Scalia, Kennedy, Thomas and Alito also struck down as exceeding the Spending Clause, Art. I, § 8, cl. 1, Congress seeking to withdraw, retroactively, state funds for States that refuse to accede to the Medicaid expansion authorized by the PPACA. See, *e.g.*, J. Rosen, "Welcome to the Roberts Court: How the Chief Justice Used Obamacare to Reveal His True Identity," *The New Republic*, June 29, 2012 ("Marshall achieved a similar act of judicial jujitsu in *Marbury v. Madison*, when he refused to confront president Jefferson over a question of executive privilege but laid the groundwork for expanding judicial power in the future.").

Republican support for his tax bill, the Omnibus Budget Reconciliation Act of 1993 in August of that year, which passed both houses of Congress without a single Republican vote. In fact, several Democratic members of Congress are said to have been certain that with their votes they were signing away their electoral prospects in November 1994. The 1993 tax law reduced taxes for almost fifteen million low-income families, expanded tax cuts for 90% of all small businesses in the United States, and — much to the annoyance of the Chamber of Commerce — increased taxes on the wealthiest 1.2% of taxpayers. This is the same law that Clinton's immediate successor President George W. Bush would repeal and which the Obama Administration is now trying to reinstate. Additionally, through the implementation of spending restraints, it mandated the budget be balanced over a number of years.

Clinton also signed the North American Free Trade Agreement (NAFTA) (applicable to the United States, Canada and Mexico) into law, after the treaty passed Congress with narrow margins in both houses. This free trade measure also established extraordinary protections for investors of one signatory from the government of another. In what are called investment treaty arbitration tribunals, run by the International Centre for the Settlement of Investment Disputes (ICSID) and a few other organizations, investors may sue for high sums of money for the direct *or* indirect expropriation of some investment. This has included situations where market share or market access has been truncated by policies of the "host State." Protectionist Democrats, anti-trade Republicans and many supporters of the Green Movement opposed NAFTA because they viewed it as weakening the regulatory power of the State to protect human rights and to maintain environmental standards.

In 1994, President Clinton pushed for and saw to the finish line his Omnibus Crime Bill, which made countless alterations to existing federal statutes. The most significant of these changes was the sweeping expansion of capital punishments to include crimes not immediately causing death, such as running a large-scale drug enterprise. During Bill Clinton's re-election campaign he asserted, "My 1994 crime bill expanded the death penalty for drug kingpins, murderers of federal law enforcement officers, and nearly 60 additional categories of violent felons." As a former constitutional law professor at the University of Arkansas Law School, Clinton must have known that this statute conflicted directly with United States Supreme Court precedent — then and now.[16] He was, however, acting as a politician now. Never taking his eye off the political ball, Clinton's "twistification" served as a "code" to the public that he understood their problems while, simultaneously, appointing reliably progressive judges to the Supreme Court and lower federal courts who would invalidate such a law. His Supreme Court appointees, Justice Ruth Bader Ginsburg and Justice Stephen Breyer, have both been quite progressive (at least more progressive than not) on criminal law and gay rights issues. After all, his 1996 re-election was

---

[16] *Kennedy v. Louisiana*, 554 U.S. 407 (2008) (there must be homicide or intended homicide in order for the death penalty to be imposed) (approvingly citing *Enmund v. Florida*, 458 U.S. 782 (1982), for the proposition that the Supreme Court "overturned the capital sentence of a defendant who aided and abetted a robbery during which a murder was committed but did not himself kill, attempt to kill, or intend that a killing would take place.").

coming up, the same reason that he signed DOMA when the Republican Congress presented him with the bill.

Governor Clinton had already acquired the nickname "Slick Willie" during his time in Arkansas, but it was during his second presidential term that he pulled off some of the greatest political escape acts. Ahead of the 1994 midterm elections, Clinton's scandals and failed healthcare initiatives left him unpopular, and the Republicans sensed their opportunity. Before November 1994, the party released a "Contract with America," vowing to cut down on government waste, work toward balancing the budget, and implementing tax reforms. That November, Clinton and the Democrats seemed to be thoroughly repudiated, as Republicans won a majority in both houses of Congress for the first time in 40 years.

The Republicans and House Speaker Newt Gingrich felt flush with power, only to soon find that Clinton was trying to co-opt the most popular aspects of the Republican Party's platform and present them as his own initiatives. And to the Republicans' chagrin, it worked. With political advisor Dick Morris, Clinton fashioned the political strategy that came to dominate his second term, "triangulation". Through this approach, Clinton would stake the middle ground between the Democrats and the Republicans and then cast himself as being the centrist and moderate, with the most sensible and level-headed positions. At the same time, Clinton took his opponent's popular policies, like balanced budgets, and owned them for himself

From 1994-1996, Gingrich and the Republicans continued to push Clinton to the brink, culminating with a government shutdown at the end of 1995. However, when the shutdown had ended, Clinton managed to come away from the political crisis with even higher popularity ratings, while Gingrich had sullied his reputation.

Clinton continued to catch the Republicans off-guard in 1996, beginning with his famous Republican-sounding talking point that "the era of big government is over." That year, Clinton embraced parts of the "Contract with America" and treated them like they were his own initiatives. Throughout the 1996 reelection campaign, the Democratic President adopted the most popular parts of the Republicans' political platforms and acted as though they were his policies. Clinton signed legislation that reduced regulations and balanced the federal budget, receiving the bulk of the credit even though the legislation had been drafted by the Republican led Congress. It seemed no matter what Republicans tried or said, Clinton deftly outmaneuvered him and used his popularity to coast to an easy victory over Senate Majority Leader Bob Dole in the 1996 presidential election.

Clinton may have announced that the "era of big government is over", but he was careful to still defend key Democratic safety net policies like Medicare and Social Security. In fact, his 1996 re-election may have hinged on his showdown with Congressional Republicans over Medicare. Republicans claimed they merely wanted to control the rate of growth of the program;

Clinton claimed they wanted to gut the program. The American people agreed with Clinton and he not only prevailed in the Medicare fight but in the 1996 election as well.

Clinton's next escape act may have been his most stunning. In January 1998, a story broke that Clinton had engaged in sexual conduct with a 22 year old White House intern, Monica Lewinsky. Clinton flatly denied the story initially, notoriously remarking, "I did not have sexual relations with that woman, Miss Lewinsky." More importantly, he had made the same claim testifying in the Paula Jones suit.

Lewinsky, however, literally had proof of the affair, which she had discussed with friend Linda Tripp, and she gave the infamous "blue dress" to special prosecutor Kenneth Starr, whose investigation had now covered everything from Whitewater to Vince Foster to Paula Jones before seemingly stumbling upon a goldmine in Lewinsky.

That July, Clinton fessed up to the affair, admitting that he had an "inappropriate relationship" with the intern, though he continued to deny that it was a "sexual relationship", at least by his understanding of that definition. The political circus truly came to town, as Americans watched the former lawyer dance through grand jury testimony, including one famous answer in which he discussed what the definition of the word "is" is. Clinton was never indicted for perjury, but he was subsequently disbarred by the state of Arkansas.

The Republican controlled Congress naturally thought Clinton had committed perjury and obstruction of justice, among other things, and began the process of impeaching the president. For only the second time in the nation's history (the first being Andrew Johnson during the Reconstruction period), the president was impeached by the U.S. House of Representatives in 1998, but eventually acquitted in the Senate after a twenty-one day trial in 1999. The nub of the charges — there were four charges in total[17] and only two (perjury and obstruction of justice) of

---

[17] H. RES. 611, U.S. House of Representatives, December 15, 1998, Article I ("On August 17, 1998, William Jefferson Clinton swore to tell the truth, the whole truth, and nothing but the truth before a Federal grand jury of the United States. Contrary to that oath, William Jefferson Clinton willfully provided perjurious, false and misleading testimony to the grand jury concerning one or more of the following: (1) the nature and details of his relationship with a subordinate Government employee; (2) prior perjurious, false and misleading testimony he gave in a Federal civil rights action brought against him; (3) prior false and misleading statements he allowed his attorney to make to a Federal judge in that civil rights action; and (4) his corrupt efforts to influence the testimony of witnesses and to impede the discovery of evidence in that civil rights action."); Article II ("(1) On December 23, 1997, William Jefferson Clinton, in sworn answers to written questions asked as part of a Federal civil rights action brought against him, willfully provided perjurious, false and misleading testimony in response to questions deemed relevant by a Federal judge concerning conduct and proposed conduct with subordinate employees. (2) On January 17, 1998, William Jefferson Clinton swore under oath to tell the truth, the whole truth, and nothing but the truth in a deposition given as part of a Federal civil rights action brought against him. Contrary to that oath, William Jefferson Clinton willfully provided perjurious, false and misleading testimony in response to questions deemed relevant by a Federal judge concerning the nature and details of his relationship with a subordinate Government employee, his knowledge of that employee's involvement and participation in the civil rights action brought against him, and his corrupt efforts to influence the testimony of that employee."); Article III ("(1) On or about December 17, 1997, William Jefferson Clinton corruptly encouraged a witness in a

them received even a majority in the Senate, let alone a super-majority (two-thirds consent of the Senate being what the Constitution requires) — was that Clinton had lied about and had asked others to lie about his improper sexual relationship with Lewinsky.

Almost unbelievably, Clinton remained extremely popular among Americans, and his approval rating hit an all time high in the days after his impeachment. In the months after Clinton admitted to the "inappropriate relationship", the Democrats picked up seats in the midterm elections, a stunning rebuke that led to the resignation of Gingrich as Speaker of the House. On February 12, 1999, the Senate acquitted Clinton on both articles of impeachment, and Clinton had managed to outlast his political opponents yet again.

In October 2000, President Clinton signed the U.S.–China Relations Act of 2000. This statute granted permanent normal trade relations (PNTR) trade status to the People's Republic of China. This was immensely pragmatic since the United States had always had friendly relations with Taiwan. Clinton now stated that free trade would gradually open China to democracy; this was

---

Federal civil rights action brought against him to execute a sworn affidavit in that proceeding that he knew to be perjurious, false and misleading. (2) On or about December 17, 1997, William Jefferson Clinton corruptly encouraged a witness in a Federal civil rights action brought against him to give perjurious, false and misleading testimony if and when called to testify personally in that proceeding. (3) On or about December 28, 1997, William Jefferson Clinton corruptly engaged in, encouraged, or supported a scheme to conceal evidence that had been subpoenaed in a Federal civil rights action brought against him. (4) Beginning on or about December 7, 1997, and continuing through and including January 14, 1998, William Jefferson Clinton intensified and succeeded in an effort to secure job assistance to a witness in a Federal civil rights action brought against him in order to corruptly prevent the truthful testimony of that witness in that proceeding at a time when the truthful testimony of that witness would have been harmful to him. (5) On January 17, 1998, at his deposition in a Federal civil rights action brought against him, William Jefferson Clinton corruptly allowed his attorney to make false and misleading statements to a Federal judge characterizing an affidavit, in order to prevent questioning deemed relevant by the judge. Such false and misleading statements were subsequently acknowledged by his attorney in a communication to that judge. (6) On or about January 18 and January 20-21, 1998, William Jefferson Clinton related a false and misleading account of events relevant to a Federal civil rights action brought against him to a potential witness in that proceeding, in order to corruptly influence the testimony of that witness. (7) On or about January 21, 23 and 26, 1998, William Jefferson Clinton made false and misleading statements to potential witnesses in a Federal grand jury proceeding in order to corruptly influence the testimony of those witnesses. The false and misleading statements made by William Jefferson Clinton were repeated by the witnesses to the grand jury, causing the grand jury to receive false and misleading information."); and Article IV ("Using the powers and influence of the office of President of the United States, William Jefferson Clinton, in violation of his constitutional oath faithfully to execute the office of President of the United States and, to the best of his ability, preserve, protect, and defend the Constitution of the United States, and in disregard of his constitutional duty to take care that the laws be faithfully executed, has engaged in conduct that resulted in misuse and abuse of his high office, impaired the due and proper administration of justice and the conduct of lawful inquiries, and contravened the authority of the legislative branch and the truth seeking purpose of a coordinate investigative proceeding, in that, as President, William Jefferson Clinton refused and failed to respond to certain written requests for admission and willfully made perjurious, false and misleading sworn statements in response to certain written requests for admission propounded to him as part of the impeachment inquiry authorized by the House of Representatives of the Congress of the United States. William Jefferson Clinton, in refusing and failing to respond and in making perjurious, false and misleading statements, assumed to himself functions and judgments necessary to the exercise of the sole power of impeachment vested by the Constitution in the House of Representatives and exhibited contempt for the inquiry.") (relevant sections and excerpts of each).

undoubtedly one place where Clinton broke with his hero John F. Kennedy's embargo on Cuba due to Fidel Castro's rule of the island. Dialogue, Clinton basically stated, is a superior force for making good on change than taking oneself out of the conversation could ever be.

Clinton's presidency has been rated highly since the moment it ended, particularly for the peacetime expansion of the American economy during his two terms. As Americans are too painfully aware now, it was under President Clinton that the United States had a projected federal budget surplus for the first time since 1969. Not even the budget hawks during the Reagan and the first President Bush presidencies could claim this particular mantle, and it promises to be a very long time before a president hands over as solid an economy as Clinton left to incoming president George W. Bush.

When Clinton was replaced in January 2001 by President Bush, he left office with the highest approval rating for an outgoing president in 40 years. As the 20th century came to a close, Clinton had much for which to be proud: he had reinvented the Democratic Party into one that was more moderate and less willing to spend money on big government programs: and he had become the first Democratic president to successfully serve out two complete terms since FDR.

Chapter 11: The Democrats Today

With President George W. Bush suffering historic lows in his approval rating during the last half of his second term, political pundits widely anticipated that the eventual Democratic nominee would be the heavy favorite to win the general election in the fall of 2008. The Republican nominee would be saddled with an unpopular incumbent, and they would be campaigning just two years after Americans had thrown Republicans out of power in the House of Representatives during midterm elections.

On January 20, 2007, Hillary announced that she was forming a presidential exploratory committee for the United States presidential election of 2008, the initial step to run for the presidency. In the announcement she boldly asserted, "I'm in, and I'm in to win." Indeed, most people thought she would, and throughout most of 2007 she was well ahead of the other known Democratic challengers in opinion polls, including former North Carolina Senator John Edwards and current Illinois Senator Barack Obama. In September, Hillary was ahead in polls in the first six states to hold primaries, and the current primary logic is that sweeping the first two in Iowa and New Hampshire generally ensures the nomination.

However, by October Hillary was starting to lose her commanding lead, brought about in part by an uncharacteristically poor debate performance. Moreover, Clinton's aura of inevitability started to work against her, as Obama began working an angle of change to counter Clinton's assurance of experience.

In the important Iowa caucus, Hillary was dealt a stinging rebuke by finishing third behind

Obama and Edwards in Iowa, and with that Obama was seen as a viable candidate. Obama gained considerable ground in national polls, and the polls indicated he would cruise to a comfortable victory in the New Hampshire primary. However, in a debate just days before, Obama made a crucial misstep by casually remarking "You're likeable enough, Hillary." And the day before the vote was held, Hillary nearly broke down while responding to a voter's question asking her how she did what she did. With tears in her eyes and her voice wavering, Hillary answered, "It's not easy, it's not easy. And I couldn't do it if I just didn't, you know, passionately believe it was the right thing to do. You know, I've had so many opportunities from this country, I just don't want to see us fall backwards - no. So - you know, this is very personal for me. It's not just political, it's not just public. I see what's happening, and we have to reverse it. And some people think elections are a game, they think it's like who's up or who's down. It's about our country, it's about our kids' futures, and it's really about all of us together. You know some of us put ourselves out there and do this against some pretty difficult odds. And we do it, each one of us, because we care about our country. But some of us are right and some of us are wrong, some of us are ready and some of us are not, some of us know what we will do to do on day one and some of haven't really thought that through enough. And so when we look at the array of problems we have and the potential for it getting - really spinning out of control, this is one of the most important elections America's ever faced. So as tired as I am - and I am - and as difficult as it is to try to kind of keep up with what I try to do on the road like occasionally exercise and try to eat right - it's tough when the easiest food is pizza - I just believe so strongly in who we are as a nation. So I'm going to do everything I can to make my case and, you know, then the voters get to decide."

All of this helped crack the façade that Clinton was an Iron Lady without emotions, and by showing herself to be human, she sprang a surprising upset victory in New Hampshire that ensured it would be a long primary.

With the primaries being close and hard fought, Clinton and Obama began to get more vicious with their attacks, which polarized the Democratic electorate. When Obama won a landslide in South Carolina on the strength of African-American votes, it was widely hailed as a victory made possible by racially charged comments made by Bill, Hillary, and other Clinton surrogates. Nevertheless, Hillary continued pressing on with her attacks on Obama, depicting him as naïve and inexperienced in debates and a famous commercial asking voters who they'd want to handle an emergency at 3:00 a.m. Hillary tried to push this difference between the two candidates, stating, "It's time that we move from good words to good works, from sound bites to sound solutions."

However, nothing Hillary could do broke the spell that Obama held over a significant bloc of Democratic voters, including minorities, young adults and college students. Obama nearly swept the primaries in February, also accruing delegates in barely contested caucus states to help bolster his delegate lead. Hillary held on in March by winning Ohio, and the following month she stayed afloat by winning Pennsylvania.

As Hillary fell further behind, she had to rely on the hopes that superdelegates would pick her despite Obama's lead in the delegate count. When it became clear that would not happen, Hillary officially conceded, despite having won more votes than Obama over the course of the campaign. In her concession speech, Hillary noted, "Although we weren't able to shatter that highest, hardest glass ceiling this time, thanks to you, it's got about 18 million cracks in it… You can be so proud that, from now on, it will be unremarkable for a woman to win primary state victories, unremarkable to have a woman in a close race to be our nominee, unremarkable to think that a woman can be the President of the United States. And that is truly remarkable."

With that, Hillary endorsed Obama and began to campaign on his behalf, helping bring her upset voters back into his tent after the bitter primary season by urging in her concession speech, "The way to continue our fight now to accomplish the goals for which we stand is to take our energy, our passion, our strength and do all we can to help elect Barack Obama."

After the Republican Party's national convention, McCain had a slight lead, but as the Great Recession began to reverberate with Bush still in office, the R next to McCain's name became too big a liability to overcome. Obama overtook McCain in the polls by September, and when Obama held his own in the presidential debates, enough Americans felt he was a safe choice.

At 10:00 p.m. on the night of November 4, 2008, the massive crowd in Grant Park exploded with joy. Barack Obama, a black man, had just been elected president. An hour later, the president-elect stepped onto a stage in the middle of Grant Park and told millions of Americans, "If there is anyone out there who still doubts that America is a place where all things are possible; who still wonders if the dream of our founders is alive in our time; who still questions the power of our democracy, tonight is your answer."

Bill Clinton once famously said that the difference between Republicans and Democrats in how they choose a candidate is that Republicans want to fall in line while Democrats want to fall in love. Unfortunately for Bill and Hillary Clinton, in 2008, Democrats fell in love with Barack Obama.

The Obama administration began with the economy in one of the worst recessions since the Great Depression. The unemployment rate hovered around 10 percent. To get the economy moving again, Obama pushed through Congress a stimulus plan. The president seemed willing to accept massive deficits and a dramatic increase in the national debt so long as the recession continued. Meanwhile, Obama embraced a muscular foreign policy and authorized the Navy Seal mission that successfully killed Osama bin Laden, the mastermind of the 9-11 terrorist attacks. He also brought the remaining American troops home from Iraq and began winding down the Afghan War.

Closer to home, Obama began working on an issue that had long been important to Democratic presidents all the way back to Truman: health care. Democrats viewed health care as a social justice issue since being sick could cost someone their entire bank account. If the philosophy of the Democrats was to use government to help people, where better than on health care? Though many Democrats supported nationalized health care, Obama settled for a Congressional plan that would require all Americans to purchase health insurance. Opponents screamed that the Commerce Clause did not allow the federal government to mandate that people buy a product. Litigation was filed and the case was soon headed to the Supreme Court. During the litigation, the Obama administration as a last resort added the argument that requiring people to buy health insurance is a tax, not a mandate. It worked. In a 5-4 decision, the Supreme Court upheld Obamacare as the law of the land.

Though the economy remained somewhat stagnant in the summer of 2012, Obama headed into re-election at the head of a Democratic Party united in its support of him and his efforts to ignite the economy and provide access to health insurance for everyone.

The journey of the Democratic Party from Jefferson to Obama has been a long and winding one. But it has generally always trended in the same direction: to being a populist party. That make up of that party has changed over the years: the Democratic coalition increasingly consists of minorities, women, union workers, academicians, and urban elites. At its best, the coalition is as committed as ever to the idea of the focusing on the employee, not the employer. The past 200 years demonstrate that sometimes the party has overreached in its creativity to find ways of using the government to assist people. The welfare state created by the 1960s asked some of the right questions (i.e., how should society help the less fortunate), but critics charge it developed too many of the wrong answers (i.e., more government spending). The Clinton era, in contrast, seemed to show that Democrats can be a populist party but not and balance the budget at the same time.

Today's Democratic Party philosophy is proudly liberal. On social issues, it embraces abortion rights, gay marriage and multiculturalism. On domestic issues, it espouses Keynesian spending initiatives to get the economy moving and invest in infrastructure. It also gets nervous that talk of entitlement reform could lead to cuts in Medicare and Social Security. And on foreign issues, it is broadly internationalist but not as convinced of American Exceptionalism as its Republican rivals. The party is now the almost exclusive home of African-American voters, as well as the home of majorities of other ethnic voters (save for Cuban-Americans). Geographically, the party is strong on both coasts and in major cities; it is much less successful in rural and heartland areas.

What does the future hold for the modern Democratic Party? As America continues to grow more racially diverse, it seems likely that the Democratic Party will continue to enjoy broad support. The party is today is more than committed than ever to its re-defined mission of using government to help the working class, and though it has long since abandoned its Jeffersonian distrust of centralized government, it remains committed to the "yeoman farmer" and the "natural aristocracy." Indeed, in many ways, Barack Obama defines the term "natural aristocrat" with his humble origins and self-made pathway to success.

Today's Democratic Party is Jeffersonian in its idealism and Rooseveltian in its foreign policy. On domestic policy, the party is sometimes divided between being Johnsonian or being Clintonian. The Obama administration has learned toward the Johnsonian path of big ideas and big spending. But an Obama second term might look different. With mounting fiscal pressures and with his last election behind him, might Obama lead the charge to save sacred Democratic programs like Medicare and Social Security by reforming them? It wouldn't be the first or the last time that the part had adjusted its philosophy to meet the demands of the times.

Made in United States
Orlando, FL
16 November 2021